AN ORDINARY GUY

WITH THE
EXTRAORDINARY GOD

THE STORY OF
FAMILY LIFE MINISTRIES/NETWORK

Dick Snavely

DEDICATED TO MY DEAR WIFE JACKIE

She has been my encourager, motivation, honest critic, lover, and help-meet. We have worked together in ministries for over fifty years. Without her partnership, there would never have been a Family Life Ministries. She has been, is, and always will be very special to me.

DEDICATED TO MY CHILDREN

Carol Anne, a Real Estate Broker and mother of two children... a son and a daughter.

Rick, my successor as President/CEO of Family Life Ministries, Inc. and father of two children... a son and a daughter.

Randy, the preacher of the family and father of four children... three sons and a daughter.

Ron, the attorney and father of three children... two daughters and a son.

ACKNOWLEDGEMENTS

THERE ARE MANY to whom I owe a deep debt of gratitude but I want to especially give thanks to:

Leigh Rumsey, who spent many hours checking and improving the manuscript. Her skillful editing work and commitment to excellence has been priceless to the publication of this book. I shall forever be grateful to Leigh for her willingness to take on such a huge task and the sacrifices she made. Leigh is librarian at the Prattsburgh Central School.

Sandy Brownlee, who provided inspiration and great encouragement to keep on keeping on with the writing. She suggested the title for the book. Sandy has authored numerous drama productions and is a writer for Family Life Ministries.

Kevin Davis, my dear computer tech buddy who used his computer skills to prepare the manuscript and graphics for electronic transmission. Without his expertise, time, and effort the book would never have seen the light of day. He is a computer expert at the Family Life Ministries/Network.

Sandy Parker, who provided inspiration and spent many hours with her eagle eyes proof reading the manuscript. In spite of her heavy work load she found time to provide this valuable service. She is Office Manager at FLM.

CONTENTS

INTRODUCTION

❧ ❧

MANY TIMES I STAND IN AWE of my Lord's blessings and I am thrilled that for some reason He allowed me, just an ordinary guy, to be a part of His workings. Often at night when I am working late and everyone is gone, I walk out into the auditorium to check doors. As I stand there I think, "Snavely, you don't have the smarts to do anything like what is happening in this ministry. To you, Oh Lord, belongs all of the glory and praise."

The thought of writing a book never occurred to me until one day, while giving a tour of the Family Life Ministries facilities. A good friend, Allen Sutfin, strongly encouraged me to put on paper the history of Youth for Christ/Family Life Ministries. He said, "Dick, you need to record the stories and miracles of how God blessed, guided and provided for this ministry over the years, because no one can tell the story like you can."

I dismissed the suggestion, knowing my limitations in writing, but for some reason I could never totally forget Allen's idea. Nearly ten years later, I began to list some of the miracles and answers to prayer that God had supplied. As I did, I became more convinced that such happenings needed to be recorded, and I told God that if He would be glorified through this book, then I would work on it.

Numerous times I abandoned this book, only to be encouraged by many friends and once again return to writing. My dear friend, Bob Abbey was always checking on my progress. He spread the word that a book was coming until it reached the point that I could not turn back because of the expectations of so many.

As I began to write, I felt like it was necessary for the reader to know a little bit about the messenger, this ordinary guy through whom God has worked. In the pages that follow, I trust you will see how, in spite of my weaknesses, failures and shortcomings, God has worked in my life and used me to accomplish His purposes. I was blessed with a godly heritage, so I can take no credit there. I was far from being the most intelligent in my class, so I had nothing of which to boast of there. I was not a little "angel" while growing up, so I can take no pride in my actions—in fact I am embarrassed by some. That is why it is easy to step aside when recognitions are given and instead give my Lord all the glory and praise. My joy is that God allowed me to play a small part in His work. I am a what-you-see-is-what-you-get type of guy. My life is an open book.

TO GOD BE THE GLORY, GREAT THINGS HE HAS DONE

"God's plan is to take ordinary people
with ordinary talents, put them into ordinary places
and then get extraordinary glory to Himself."
Dr. Adrian Rogers

PART I

PREPARATION

1

❧ ❧

IN THE BEGINNING

"The lines are fallen unto me in pleasant places;
yea, I have a godly heritage."
Psalm 16:6 ASV

A GODLY HERITAGE

IT ALL BEGAN as just another ordinary autumn day on the Snavely farm. The air was nippy as the family rose early that morning to do their usual chores. The chickens were fed, the eggs gathered, the pigs slopped and the cows milked. Most of the summer crops had already been harvested and neatly stored for the long winter.

Events that day began to take on extraordinary significance and excitement when word spread that the lady of the house had developed birth pangs. The day was Friday, November 15, 1907. The location was the old red brick Snavely farm house located on a gravel road south of Strasburg in Lancaster County, Pennsylvania. The event was the birth of a bouncing baby boy. The proud parents were Amos Herr and Lizzie Herr Snavely. They named the healthy round-faced child Abram Herr Snavely. He was one of two boys and four girls to be born to this Mennonite family. Twenty-four years later, in the very same farmhouse, that baby boy would become my father.

Dad spent his first twenty-nine years on that dairy farm. It was there that he learned how to work and accept responsibilities. Unbeknown to him, God was working in his life and developing character. He and his siblings walked down the road about a mile to school every day. In that small, one-room brick school house, Dad completed his formal education after the eighth grade since he was needed to work the farm.

Years later, Dad met a beautiful young lady and courted her for some time. A few days before his 24th birthday, Abram Herr Snavely married Anna Mary Mellinger. Within a year they started their own family. Mother gave birth to me on Thursday, June 4, 1931. Eighteen months later, my sister Marian was born. Four years later, my brother Glenn came into this world. Their fourth child, James, was born in 1940 but died five months later from pneumonia.

That old farmhouse is unique in that it still stands today as a three-story, double house which was built in the 1770's. At one time slaves were housed in the attic, and the wooden posts to which their chains were fastened are still visible. As a double house, it provided an ideal setting for the extended family. Grandpa and Grandma Snavely lived on one side and our family on the other. The first five years of my life were spent on this farm, where I received tender loving care from both my parents and grandparents.

Grandma Snavely was a skinny little lady who weighed no more than ninety-eight pounds soaking wet. Even though she was an elderly grandmother, she liked the action and speed of riding with Cousin Benny Landis in his 1941 Chevy. She was a lively one, although nearly deaf. She wore a hearing aid, which in those days consisted of a microphone hung around her neck and connected by wires to an earplug. She joked around with the grandchildren, often acting like she couldn't hear what they were saying. They in turn would whisper, forcing her to turn up the volume. Then they would yell. She would jump and laugh while shaking her index finger at them. There were times when she acted like she couldn't hear anything, but I am sure she heard many things that others did not want her to hear.

During the last years of her life, Grandma lived with Uncle Paul and Aunt Blanche Meck, her daughter, on their farm south of Strasburg. I remember visiting her while she lay sick on her bed and when she died, wondering if I would ever see her again. I hoped, but had no reason for my hope.

I vaguely remember sitting on Grandpa's knee while rocking in his chair next to the old wood stove in the kitchen. He was known in the community as a kind and godly man with a gentle spirit. Every Sunday morning, he and our entire family attended the Strasburg Mennonite Church. It was at this Mennonite church that I received my early religious instruction.

BIG MOVE TO A SMALL FARM

At age sixty, Grandpa Snavely suffered a heart attack and died. This was a tragic blow to Grandma and the family. As the eldest son, Dad wanted to farm the old homestead. His sisters insisted on selling it. The farm was a sense of security for Dad and losing it forced him out of his comfort zone. He was discouraged and admitted that he lacked self-confidence as he faced the challenging crossroads in his life. Although he didn't know it, God was at work in his life through adversity. Adversities and adversaries can become victories and friends when we commit them to the Lord.

God also works through encouraging words. With his own father now gone and with the responsibilities of a young family, Dad was unsure of his future. He often told me how he was inspired by the words of his Uncle Harry Snavely, who saw great potential in Dad and encouraged him to strike out on his own. Uncle Harry was well known in Lancaster County political circles as H.H. Snavely, the County Treasurer. Dad rose to the challenge, struck out on his own, and bought a small farm between Neffsville and Lititz, next to the Lancaster County airport.

I was five years old when we moved from the old Snavely homestead in Strasburg to a much smaller thirteen acre farm in Lancaster County. I well remember this old house because it lacked plumbing and a bathroom. We had an outhouse that we used during daytime hours. It was a two-seater, but I never remember more than one seat being occupied at a time. It was there that I was introduced to the Sears Roebuck catalogue, which was used for purposes in this outhouse that I'm sure Mr. Sears and Mr. Roebuck had never intended. For nighttime emergencies we used chamber buckets that were kept under the beds. As the oldest of four children, one of my responsibilities was to empty those buckets every morning. It was one job I did not like.

My other chores on the farm included carrying firewood, collecting eggs, feeding the livestock, mowing the lawn, and carrying out the ashes from the old coal furnace. Every Monday, Mother would wash the clothes and since there was no plumbing in the house, I would carry buckets of wash water from the house out to the ditch by the side of the road. Dad worked hard to remodel that old house and we were all happy when he finally gave us the luxury of indoor plumbing and a real bathroom.

Mother was also a hard worker and a good cook. She prepared all of our meals on the old wood stove. She assisted in the barn work from time to time as well. She carried many burdens and concerns for her family as any good mother would. I knew she loved me and my siblings.

My second brother James was born shortly after we moved to this smaller farm. Mother had a difficult childbirth with Jimmy and had to have a Cesarean section. Five months after he was born, Jimmy took ill. I saw my mother rock that little baby for many hours as he struggled with pneumonia. Finally he fought for his last breath and the Lord took him home. I remember seeing him suffer and then seeing his body in a casket. If penicillin were available to us at that time, I believe Jimmy would have survived. But God had different plans and taught our family many lessons through our loss. At that time, I had no idea if I would ever see my brother again. I hoped, but as one who had no hope.

God blessed me with a great heritage. Through these childhood experiences He was preparing and equipping me for life.

2

❦ ❦

MY DAD

MY FATHER WAS a great influence in my life as I tried to follow in his footsteps as a child. I often heard him speak of how he was influenced by his godly father and I have often prayed that someday I would be the same godly influence for my children. Even though he was a religious man and attended church faithfully, he had not yet experienced God's forgiveness and the grace and mercy of the Lord Jesus Christ. Dad was a hard worker and had great character, but he was not yet the man he was going to become.

He gave me responsibilities as a young lad and taught me many farm chores. Dad always expected my jobs to be done well and in a timely fashion. I could expect some stern discipline if my chores were neglected. Later in life I came to appreciate the strong work ethic that I learned from him. Dad's famous slogan was "Good, better, best. Never let it rest until your good is better and your better best."

THE ENTREPRENEUR

Dad was always on the cutting edge when it came to new ideas and products. One day he came home with a hi-fi system that cut grooves in plastic records. We kids sang and talked into the microphone while Dad recorded us. Every time a relative came for a visit we would show off this record cutter. It was fun to hear our voices coming out of that speaker. The next recording device to hit the market was a Webcor wire recorder. Sure enough, Dad bought one and we recorded everything within earshot. We had a lot of fun until the steel wire got tangled on the spool and then it was a nightmare.

Even though the church was against it, we were one of the first homes in our town to get a television set. Our favorite program was Howdy Doody.

One day Dad said that he wanted me to see a new automobile that was ahead of its time with many innovative ideas. I was excited as Dad and I traveled to Mount Joy to see the Tucker automobile on display. Dad had bought stock in the Tucker automobile company and was slated to be a dealer, but the competition in Detroit saw to it that it never got off the ground.

Dad's entrepreneurial spirit became very evident as he struggled to support his family of six. Because the farm was small, he had to seek additional income. He was one of the first farmers in Lancaster County to purchase a farm tractor with rubber tires and an Ann Arbor hay baler. He began working long hours every summer travelling countywide from farm to farm with his modern agricultural equipment doing custom work for area farmers.

In the late 1930's, two brothers by the name of Sensenig bought several acres of the farm. They built a factory where they manufactured wooden airplane propellers and Dad became one of their first employees. They enrolled him in night school where he took college courses in many subjects, including time study management. This involved studying the time it took a worker to carve different sections of the wooden propeller and then looking for ways to increase the productivity of each carver. Although he had never graduated from high school, Dad was an excellent student and ultimately secured more credits than needed for a college degree. He also took flying lessons and became a pilot, much to my mother's chagrin.

When the United States got involved in World War II, the propeller factory bought more land from Dad and increased the production of airplane propellers for the war effort.

WORLD WAR II

The date of December 7, 1941 left an indelible mark on my memory. Our family had just returned home from church when we heard about the Japanese attack on Pearl Harbor. I was ten years old and terrified. All I could think of was death and destruction, and the pictures in the newspapers confirmed my fears. I remember putting my ear down next to Dad's at the speaker of the old radio to listen to the news commentator's report. It became a ritual every evening, listening to Gabriel Heater's reports on the war effort and Drew Pearson, who was known for his news predictions. I would anxiously look at the war map every day with my Dad. The front page of the newspaper would show the progress of the allied troops in Europe and the reports of the fighting with Japan.

The war created more anxiety for me when the fire sirens would blast away warning us of a possible air raid. When the sirens sounded at night we had to turn off all lights and wait in darkness. There were many air raid drills and we never knew if this was the real one or not. Since the propeller factory worked shifts around the clock, all of the windows in the building were painted black to keep the light from shining through. Living between an airport and the airplane propeller factory made us feel like a real target in the event of an attack.

Dad's younger brother, my Uncle Ben, was living with us and was called up for his army physical exam. He was ready to report for duty when suddenly a deferment came through because he was a defense worker at the propeller factory. I was fearful about the strong possibility of Dad being drafted into the Army. Would he leave home? How long would he be gone? Would he get shot and killed? How could we live without him? Being a Mennonite, he would have been expected to go as a conscientious objector, which meant that he would have had to serve time somewhere in a non-combative assignment. Thankfully, that never came to be.

MY FIRST BUSINESS

Around the age of nine, I became an entrepreneur. I sold shoe laces, greeting cards, flower and vegetable seeds, magazine subscriptions, and anything else that would earn a little extra money. Then Dad built me a wagon with which I hauled a large icebox filled with soft drinks and chocolate milk to sell to the propeller factory employees. I did this twice a day during the summer. Since vending machines were not popular in that era, I really had a monopoly on the refreshment business. After a few weeks, we decided to expand my business by adding another line of products. We began making an earlier trip through the factory selling salty peanuts, potato chips, and cookies. Needless to say, sales in soft drinks soared in direct proportion to the thirst factor.

In this way, Dad taught me many things involved in operating a small business. He set me up with a budget using envelopes for such items as clothing, savings, charity, and miscellaneous spending. He showed me how to make a profit, although I did eat and drink a lot of the profits that Dad never saw. I always made certain that I had enough money to meet my next bill with the soft drink company. I learned how to save, spend, and give to the Lord's work.

In grade school I was involved in 4-H clubs. While most boys chose projects such as raising animals, I opted for the food canning projects, fueled by my attraction to the number of girls in the class. As the only boy, I was a celebrity and had reporters come to our house to photograph me with my many jars of preserved vegetables. One summer I canned—with the help of my dear, patient mother—forty quarts of vegetables.

For the next several years my 4-H project was raising tobacco on a portion of a field on our small farm. Tobacco was a very good cash crop and I banked some good money for my effort. It was a year-round job. With Dad's help, I planted the seed in hot beds in the spring and later transplanted the seedlings into the field. I had to keep the many rows of tobacco plants cultivated with a hoe to keep the weeds out. I disliked pulling weeds and one time when Dad saw the weeds higher than the tobacco plants, I felt the impression of the hoe handle on my backside for several days. The weeds never again got out of control. The tobacco plants needed to be topped and succored for the plants to develop broad leaves. This was all done by hand. After the tobacco plants were fully grown, we cut the individual stalks of tobacco, strung them on laths, and hung them in the barn to cure. Next came the job of pulling the leaves from the stalks, sizing them according to the different lengths, tying them in small bundles, and finally baling them. This work in the tobacco cellar was called stripping tobacco and lasted most of the winter. Many members of the family joined in from time to time. This time-consuming job was enhanced by the many stories and jokes we would share around an old potbelly stove that kept us warm. Many evenings of good fellowship were spent stripping tobacco through the cold winter months.

In all of these little businesses with shoe laces, soft drinks, greeting cards, and tobacco, God was preparing me for His business in the future. Even though I was unaware of it at the time, God had a plan for my life.

3

❧ ❧

CHILDHOOD EXPERIENCES

ENTERTAINMENT

As a curious lad, I decided to make my own cigar one afternoon when no one was in the tobacco cellar. I took one leaf and chopped it up to use as filler. Then I used another leaf to wrap it. It was a crude-looking cigar, but I was able to get it lit. After the first drag I nearly choked to death. I took several more drags, thinking I was a big shot. I began to feel a little dizzy as I sat down by the old pig pen. My stomach began to churn and then I heard Mother calling me for supper. Food did not look appealing and I had to confess to my mother why my appetite was gone.

Another form of entertainment—at least I thought it was entertainment at the time—really got me into a lot of trouble. I could never explain why I did such a foolish thing. One day when I was about nine years old, I was out in back of the barn when I got the strongest urge to hear glass shatter. I knew better, but gave in to the temptation. So I picked up some stones and threw them at the windows in the chicken house. When I scored a direct hit, the glass would crack and the chickens inside would go berserk. I continued to throw stones and smash those windows until every glass pane was shattered. I don't think those chickens laid very many eggs that day. I still don't know what possessed me to smash those windows, but to this very day I love the sound of shattering glass.

That evening I went to bed early since Dad was going to take me into Lancaster the next morning to buy me an accordion. While trying to fall asleep, I heard Dad talking with someone downstairs and I went over to the stove pipe opening in the floor to hear. To my horror, it was our neighbor telling Dad that he ought to check his chicken house. From across the field, he had witnessed me smashing those windows. I knew I was in deep trouble. After he left, Dad came upstairs, told me to get dressed and led me out to the chicken house. There was glass all over the place and he asked me if I knew anything about it. I confessed.

It was a confession I shall never forget because Dad led me down inside the barn and picked up a tobacco lath on the way. He applied that wooden lath to my backside in such a way that over sixty years later I still have those memories. It ended what I thought was entertainment and I have never intentionally broken any windows since that day. It also ended my music career since I never did get that accordion the next day as planned.

Broken glass and cigars aside, most of our fun was harmless. I had many wonderful childhood experiences with my brother Glenn and sister Marian. Mother used to get upset when Glenn and I got the boxing gloves out and began boxing on our bed. I would get on my knees since I was taller, and we would box until the bed slats fell out, the box spring and mattress came crashing down, and Mother came upstairs to read us the riot act.

Living next to the Lancaster County Airport, my siblings and I found a lot of excitement in sitting at the edge of our yard and watching airplanes take off and land. We found additional diversion by watching people take their test for their Pennsylvania driver's license. The entrance road to the airport was in front of our house and was used by the Pennsylvania State Police to test the new applicants' driving skills. We would watch with anticipation as a new applicant would have to turn his car around in the middle of the road. Automatic transmissions were not in vogue those days and we would hear engines roar, clutches slip, and tires squeal as drivers would jerk forward and backward. The head of the testing policeman would jerk forward and backward as well, while some very inexperienced drivers would pop the clutch and hit the brakes.

One such examinee gave us an especially hearty laugh when he forgot to use his brakes at all and went over the embankment with the policeman hanging on. It was cheap entertainment for us but we found it very amusing. Not only did those poor student drivers have to contend with the examining police officer sitting by them in the car, but they also had to endure my sister Marian, brother Glenn and me laughing up a storm.

Mother was a very patient mother. She really put up with a lot when we were kids. I know we embarrassed her at times with our shenanigans. Whenever the local Christian Business Men's Committee sponsored an evangelistic crusade in the county, Dad would invite the visiting evangelist or pastor for dinner at our house. Glenn and I had our little tricks that we liked to play on these unsuspecting clergy. Glenn had a plastic ice cube with a fly in the center that he would place in the preacher's glass of water when Mother was not looking. We had a hard time keeping a straight face, and sometimes the preacher would give us a dirty look when he saw Glenn snickering, but, at other times they would go along with the joke. Mother apologized and then scolded us after dinner.

One afternoon, our family invited some missionaries for lunch. I planted a balloon under the table cloth and dinner plate of one missionary. Connected to this small balloon was a piece of rubber tubing which was connected to a rubber bulb that I held in my hand to pump air into the balloon. As the missionary took his fork to begin eating, I would squeeze the bulb and his dinner plate would rise up and down. Glenn and I would smile and act innocent, but Mother would give us the dirty look, and we knew we'd be washing the dishes again.

We really got into trouble when we put hard, dried marshmallows in Mother's blender. It made a terrible racket and bent the rotating knives. We recorded it on the wire recorder, announcing to the world that this was the Russian's latest machine gun.

Sunday school was another place where our mischievousness could often be seen. We would catch flies, then pull off pieces of thread from the lining of our pants pockets and tie them to the leg of the flies. Once released, the flies looked like little airplanes trailing a sign behind. This was quite a grand distraction.

THIRD GRADE DISASTER

I attended grade school at Manheim Township School in Neffsville, PA. My third grade year in that school greatly altered my personality because I was punished many times for something I never did.

Esther, a fellow classmate whose desk was next to mine, would write nasty notes about the teacher, then would give these notes to the teacher and tell her that I wrote them. The teacher would question me, and even though I denied it she would punish me by spanking me in front of my classmates. I cried and felt foolish in front of my peers. This went on for what seemed like months. I became fearful, lonely, and very nervous. I felt that no one understood me or believed me.

One day, in desperation, I finally agreed and told the teacher that I did write one of the notes, even though it was a lie. It didn't appease her and I still got the spanking in front of my classmates. The notes continued to come. One day the teacher decided to

send me to the principal who was teaching a class of eighth graders. The principal made me stand in front of the eighth grade
class and hold out my hands. With a ruler, he hit my fingers until
I cried and then made me sit in the back of the room and copy a
lesson word for word from the history book.

I hated to go to school. I was afraid to tell my parents because they always warned me that if I ever got a spanking in
school, I would also get one at home. I felt trapped and looked
for a way out. One spring day while walking home from the bus
stop, I found some poison ivy and thought that getting a rash
would be a good excuse to keep me out of school. I plucked some
of the leaves and rubbed them all over my arms, legs and face.
The next day that poison ivy came out all over my body. I was
one miserable kid, but it worked. I did not have to go to school
for the next few days.

Mother and Dad were alarmed and questioned where I could
have gotten such a bad case of poison ivy. After some questioning and much crying, I told them that I was getting spanked at
school for something I never did. I told them I was afraid of
school. They immediately understood and Dad encouraged me
to keep telling the truth.

The next day Dad went to school and spoke to the teacher.
After looking at some of the notes, he informed her that he was
confident that his son did not write them because he knew that
his son had never heard some of those words. Miss Hess asked
Esther and me to go to the blackboard for a little test. I miss-
pelled the word "sh--", and it finally dawned on her that I was
not the author of the dirty notes. That was one time it paid to be
a poor speller.

Esther admitted that she was the one who had been writing
those notes for those many weeks and blaming me. She was removed from the classroom and got her spanking. That afternoon
Miss Hess took us both home from school and explained all that
had happened and apologized to my mother. Miss Hess also

made Esther apologize. She then took Esther to her home and informed her parents of the incidents. I believe Miss Hess tried to reconcile matters with me because the next day she removed Esther's desk from beside mine and placed her in the corner of the room. Then, she moved the cutest girl in the class next to me for the remainder of the year.

Although I was vindicated, the damage had been done. For the next several years I became a very bashful kid in school. My personality was very subdued and I never felt like I was a real part of my class. I felt like I was the underdog and the one who was always getting stomped on.

REBELLION

During my 8th grade year, the Sensenig brothers needed more room to expand their factory and growing business and they wanted to buy more farmland from Dad. Since they already had purchased the best part of the farmland, Dad would not sell unless they bought the entire farm. Finally, an agreement was reached and Dad sold the remainder of the farm.

Again, Dad made another bold move by purchasing a farm machinery and small appliance business in Blue Ball, Pennsylvania. The business was a dealership with Allis Chalmers and Case farm equipment. He later asked his brother, my Uncle Ben, to join him and they named the business Snavely's Farm Service.

This business venture necessitated a move to another community. I would be entering a totally new school and the situation did not look good to me. Blue Ball was a small community. I would be moving from a large school system which included all of the twelve grades to a small two-room school house with eight grades.

As the new teenager in town, I was not immediately accepted. Some of the tough guys in town were led by Flap

Townsley. I don't know why they called him Flap, other than the fact that he had big ears. He did not want me invading his turf, so he set out to beat me up. I was scared. One day, when Dad asked me to go get the mail, I told him that I was afraid of the big boys in town. He went to town with me. I walked confidently by his side smiling while the tough boys watched me. I was not afraid until the next day when I had to go for the mail by myself. Flap saw me enter the grocery store which also accommodated the post office. I was afraid to leave because I knew that he and several of his followers were waiting for me.

Finally, I got up the courage to face my bully. I walked out onto the porch. Flap came nose to nose with me, spouting all kinds of threats. I thought he was going to hit me so I decided to hit him first. I punched him in the mouth and ran for my bike. I headed out the path at the back of the store with Flap and his cohorts chasing me. I did not get very far before they ditched me and piled on me with their fists flying. That one-minute fight marked the beginning of my acceptance by the guys of Blue Ball.

My behavior was anything but exemplary in Blue Ball's two-room schoolhouse. I remember telling myself that I was now in a new school where no one knew me and I was going to be the tough guy. I determined that no one was going to push me around, including the teacher, so I gave her a very difficult time.

Miss Gehman, my new teacher, was a spinster and had been teaching grades five to eight for many years. I caused her terrible grief and consternation. I would provoke fights in the library, which consisted of a few shelves of books in the back of the room. One day while Miss Gehman was teaching the fifth graders, I asked a classmate to meet me in the library and hit me. I yelled bloody murder, disturbing the teacher and causing all of the students in the other grades to snicker and look to the back of the room. I received the attention and result that I wanted. Miss Gehman yelled at me and we then got into a shouting match.

It was very much out of character for me to speak to an adult in such a manner. I never spoke to my parents or any other adult the way I talked to this teacher. I would make noises while she was teaching in another part of the room just to get a reaction from her. She was ready to throw chalk at me if she thought I was making the noise. I enjoyed agitating her.

One day while school was in session, I was whistling softly while the teacher was in the back of the room. My desk was at the front of the room and my fellow classmate, Roy Burkholder, sat across the aisle. As I softly whistled, I watched Miss Gehman slowly come up from the back of the room to the area where she thought the whistling was coming from. Roy Burkholder was slouched down in his desk chair and engrossed in reading a book. As she got closer and closer, I stopped and watched her out of the corner of my eye. All of a sudden she banged Roy on the top of his head with a book and yelled at him. Poor Roy never knew what was happening and really got the surprise of his life. I don't know if she ever knew that she hit the wrong person, but I enjoyed the little prank.

I really looked forward for my turn to ring the old school bell on top of the school. At the beginning of the day and at each recess, we would ring the bell by pulling on a rope suspended from the ceiling. I did not have many opportunities to ring that bell because several times I deliberately pulled extra hard on the rope and then let it go up through the ceiling, thus upsetting the bell on the roof. Miss Gehman soon suspended me from bell-ringing duties.

It was not until adulthood, as I reflected on these incidents, that I realized that poor Miss Gehman was paying for the resentment that I felt toward my third grade teacher. At the end of the school year, Miss Gehman informed me that I narrowly passed the eighth grade. I truly believe she promoted me to the ninth grade only because she did not want me around for another year.

Upon my graduation from the two-room school in Blue Ball, I began the first of my four years at New Holland High School. I would often find a ride or hitchhike to school. Being a freshman in a big high school, I reverted back to my bashful and shy ways. I did very little dating socially as I was extremely self-conscious of my terrible acne problem. I had a very negative self-image.

I took the business/commercial course because it seemed to be the easiest route to a high school diploma. I studied just enough to pass each year, so I was a very poor student. I did not participate in many activities in high school, but I played briefly on the junior varsity basketball team and did some running on the track team.

All through my high school years I worked at my Dad's business after school and during the summer months. While this limited my participation in sports, in trade I received valuable experience in the various aspects of his business. One summer I worked with the mechanics in the shop and the next summer in the parts department. Other times I worked in sales or in the office with bookkeeping and records. It was an excellent education to prepare me to be a partner in the business. These experiences were far more exciting to me than school books.

CAR TROUBLE

While growing up, I grabbed every opportunity I could to drive Dad's car around the farm. I know Dad regretted allowing me to back the car out of the barn one Sunday morning. I was the first one ready for church and I begged Dad to let me pull the car out of the barn. Reluctantly, he handed over the keys. The double doors to the barn were typically difficult to open, but on that day one of those doors would not budge. I struggled with it knowing that if I didn't get it open before Dad came out, I would not be able to drive the car. So, in my eagerness, I decided I could get the car out with only one door open. I did, but not without some scratches. Dad was very unhappy, but since we were on our way to church, I got a reprieve.

Another incident in which I got a reprieve was one sunny Sunday afternoon when our family visited Uncle Paul and Aunt Blanche Meck's farm. While our parents were visiting in the house, cousin Melvin hatched an adventuresome idea. To this day he claims it was my suggestion, but that is still up for debate. The idea was to take a spin in the old pickup truck used around the farm. Although Melvin was younger and shorter than I, he would be the driver. After all, it was his farm, his truck and his idea—I think.

Melvin crawled into the driver's seat, hardly able to see over the dashboard. His foot barely reached the clutch, and he could not see out of the windshield and touch the brake and gas pedals at the same time. I climbed aboard on the passenger's side, ready to give Melvin visual suggestions because at least I could see where we were headed.

He backed the truck up, preparing to head up the hill past the barn and toward the long lane. Melvin was very proficient with shifting gears which gave us a good running start up that hill. The driveway had two large speed bumps to divert water during rainstorms. When we hit that first speed bump, Melvin was able to get a good glimpse of where we were headed since he bounced up in the air off of the driver's seat. About the time he came back down we hit the second speed bump. He was losing control but we were really moving.

Our next challenge was to navigate a left hand turn onto that long lane. At our current speed, Melvin realized that we could not make it. Another alternative was to turn right and head down the cow trail to the barn. I was hanging on, not knowing what to expect when I realized that *any* turn would be impossible. With the pickup truck now completely out of control, we headed straight into a very large post. We hit with a thud, so hard that a box of shotgun shells that was sitting in the back window flew past my head and landed on the ground in front of the truck.

When the dust settled we looked at each other and then got out to assess the damage. The headlight was smashed backwards and the bumper was pushed in. The damage did not seem to be too extensive until we tried to drive the truck. We could not turn the wheels very far so we had to back up the truck and creep forward, repeating this process many times. Finally, we were able to get the truck back to its original place.

Everything looked normal because Melvin pulled the truck up against the barn door to hide the damage. We discussed briefly how to explain what happened. We could have made all kinds of excuses but we knew the Bible says, *"Be sure your sins will find you out."* It was not until the next day, after I was gone, that Melvin was confronted by his Dad regarding the broken headlight and then the whole truth was revealed. I knew Uncle Paul was gracious in his discipline because Melvin lived to relate this story many times.

Turning sixteen was the fulfillment of a dream and the highlight of my young life. Although I had been driving tractors and Dad's car around the barnyard for years, now I could get my official driver's license. I applied for my permit a week ahead of my 16th birthday. My birthday was June 4th, my driver's permit arrived on the 5th, and I took my driving test on the 6th, and passed with flying colors.

I gained a new freedom and power with that driver's license. Now I was somebody. I drove Dad's car whenever I could. Racing was in my blood. I loved to challenge other guys to race down the back road. I was referred to as one of the Mennonite cowboys in the area as we would race our cars and spin our wheels to burn rubber and show off.

God, in His mercy, spared me from any accidents. I often look back on my life and realize that but for the mercy and grace of God, I should have had many fatal collisions. In my high school senior book my classmates nicknamed me the "Blue Streak," referring to my Dad's blue Chrysler.

With the recent end of World War II, new cars were difficult to acquire, but as a senior in high school, I bought a brand new 1949 Pontiac. It was fully loaded with all of the extras such as a sun visor, spot light, radio, under seat heater, fender skirts, white wall tires, a lighted Indian-head hood ornament, hydromatic transmission, fog lights, and grill guard. The total price for my fully loaded two-door dark blue 1949 Pontiac sedan was less than $2,500. I was able to pay most of it in cash from my savings from my entrepreneurial ventures. Dad co-signed a bank loan for the balance which I paid off in a few months. I practically worshipped that car. I washed it, raced it and showed it off. Now, over fifty years later, I still carry the picture of that car in my wallet, but it is no longer my god.

Twice my driver's license was revoked for reckless driving. To make an arrest for speeding, a police officer had to follow for a certain distance to record speed on his speedometer. Since the police were never able to follow me in that way, I was arrested for reckless driving. I really was a nuisance. To make as much noise as possible, I cut one end off my muffler and removed all of the interior baffles. With a gutted muffler, the sound of an eight-cylinder engine really purred. It got extra loud when I pulled the hydromatic transmission into a lower gear, turned off the engine for a few seconds while cruising and then turned it on again. The result was a loud bang with fire shooting out of the muffler. The town cop sure didn't look favorably upon this.

During one license suspension, a truck driver friend suggested that he could get me a driver's license and license plates on his next trip to Georgia. In this way, I thought I would be able to legally continue driving while my Pennsylvania driver's license was suspended. I found out later that it doesn't work that way. The truck driver returned from Georgia with the driver's license and license plate registered for my car. He had used a Georgia gas station for my address. I thought I was really cool until I was informed that an all-county bulletin had been radioed to the Pennsylvania State Police for my arrest.

My Uncle Bill Mellinger, who was a foreman at the Packard auto garage in Lancaster, called Dad and said that a state trooper had told him about this Snavely kid in Blue Ball who was driving with illegal plates. Dad immediately told me to stay off the highway and to get rid of those Georgia plates. When I saw the state police cruising around the parking area at my Dad's business, I knew my driving freedom was over and I immediately gave my car to my girlfriend to do all of the driving until my license suspension expired. A few days later, two state policemen came to Dad's business while I was working and questioned me about the Georgia license plates. I told them the truth about everything and that I was unaware that what I had done was illegal. They informed me that I would have been headed for jail if they had caught me on the highway. Oh, how foolish this seventeen year old kid was.

4

⧼ ⧽

A NEW DIMENSION

DAD'S EXPERIENCE

IN 1948, MY DAD'S LIFE and destiny changed forever. For several years Dad had been searching for something that he could not put his finger on. That feeling was intensified by attending the Lancaster County Christian Businessmen's Committee meetings where he heard men stand up and publicly profess their faith in Jesus Christ. He knew some of these men and their past lives. One such man who had committed adultery now talked about his assurance of going to heaven when he died because of God's forgiveness. Dad could not understand such forgiveness and assurance, but he knew that these men had something that he lacked.

Dad continued to attend the CBMC meetings and many times heard the men quote a verse of Scripture that had real meaning for them personally. Dad thought that their testimonies were acts of pride, and when he was called upon he would quote the verse *"Pride goeth before destruction and a haughty spirit be-*

fore a fall." Still, he sensed that something was real with these men and that maybe something was missing in his life.

One day, Dad called on the pastor of the Mennonite church we attended. He suggested to Dad that these CBMC meetings were the cause of his confusion. He counseled him to stop attending the meetings and to become more devoted to the local church. Dad began wearing the plain suit which was the Mennonite dress for men and contributing more money from the business, but these changes did not satisfy the spiritual hunger that Dad felt. In fact, after complying with the pastor's requests, his hunger and thirst for deeper spiritual meaning intensified.

Dad's early instruction in doctrine had led him to believe that one could never be sure of heaven until he stood before the great Judge, God Himself. He was afraid to accept not only the assurance of salvation through Christ, but also the keeping power of Christ. The doctrine of "once saved, always saved" was considered a damnable belief in our household. We were taught that such assurance would be a license to sin.

At the invitation of a CBMC businessman, Dad attended a spiritual life conference at America's Keswick in New Jersey. One afternoon on the hotel porch overlooking a beautiful lake, Dad became engrossed in a conversation with Mr. Clark Hildebrand, a State Farm Life Insurance agent from York, PA. Mr. Hildebrand wanted to explain to Dad the grace, mercy and keeping power of Jesus Christ. He knew that Dad did not believe in eternal security, so before they began their discussion, he asked Dad if he would agree not to argue with him but rather accept these truths of forgiveness and eternal life if they could be proven from the Bible. Dad agreed.

The insurance agent took his Bible and began to show Dad in the Scriptures the love of Jesus Christ and how God unconditionally adopts us into His family through faith in Him. He showed Dad in Ephesians 2:8-9, how forgiveness for our sins and eternal salvation is attained by His grace, through faith, and not of ourselves, but that it is a gift of God and it is not of our works lest we should boast. It was a truth that Dad had always been taught to reject. Instead, he had been taught that one must do good works and hopefully be good enough to get into heaven. Dad lived in fear of death and eternity because of the unknown and was always afraid that he would not be good enough to enter heaven. He could not accept the "gift" idea, and that once received it would never be taken away.

Dad began to argue with the insurance agent only to be reminded that he was actually arguing with God's Word. All of a sudden Dad said, "I see" and his spiritual blindness was ended. His eyes were opened; the Holy Spirit revealed Truth to Dad and Dad believed it. Immediately he excused himself and went to his room with Mother. Together they fell upon their knees and Dad cried out to God. He confessed to God that he was a sinful man. He confessed that he believed that Jesus Christ died on the cross to pay the penalty for his sins and asked for God's forgiveness. He also thanked God for his eternal salvation and the assurance that God would keep Him and never forsake him. He made a commitment to live for Jesus Christ after all God had done for him. Mother, in her quiet and unassuming manner, had already committed her life to the Lord years earlier.

Afterwards, Dad often talked about the load that had been lifted from him when he yielded and by faith accepted Christ as the One who died and rose again to pay the payment for his sins. By faith he trusted Christ as his Savior and by faith he trusted in Him to keep him from falling. It was quite an emotional experience that day. For forty-one years he had walked in darkness, fear, and bondage only to be set free for all eternity.

That Sunday afternoon Mother and Dad walked into the Keswick Bible Conference tabernacle shortly after the meeting had started. I saw them coming down the aisle and noticed that Dad's eyes were red. I knew he was weeping and I knew something drastic had happened. As they sat down in their pew, the song leader was leading the congregation in song—"Amazing Grace, how sweet the sound that saved a wretch like me. I once was lost but now I'm found, was blind but now I see." I looked at Dad and he began to cry like a baby. The words of that song described exactly what he had just experienced.

As an inquisitive teenager, I remember observing the discussion my Dad was having with that insurance man on the front porch that afternoon. The man had his Bible open and was explaining the Scripture verses to my Dad. I was very puzzled. I had been taught that life insurance was of the devil because it evidenced a lack of faith and trust in the Lord. He also wore a wedding ring. Jewelry was very worldly according to our church doctrine. I was certain that the insurance agent was headed to hell. These were evil things, yet it was very evident that the insurance agent had a greater knowledge of the Scripture than my Dad. How could this be? My early indoctrination made it difficult for me to understand how this insurance man could ever be a Christian.

DAD'S INFLUENCE

Things changed dramatically in our household. Dad began to have Bible reading every morning at the breakfast table. Things changed at the business. Dad conducted Bible studies every morning with his employees after they checked in for work. Salesmen were confronted with the Gospel. Dad shared his faith in Jesus Christ with every customer he could. At times his office became a counseling room instead of a sales room. Often, instead of closing a deal, he closed with prayer after leading a man to Christ.

Dad's faith was contagious. I watched. I was impressed. I was influenced. His hunger for truth and Biblical knowledge consumed him. He enrolled in the Scofield Bible Correspondence

School and attended evening classes. He began memorizing the Bible and ended up memorizing over five hundred verses through the Navigators Bible Memory program. He memorized while driving the car. To the chagrin of us kids, he memorized while sitting in the bathroom while the rest of the family waited.

His conversion caused quite a stir in our church and some heated discussions with our relatives. Everyone knew that Dad had "something," and friends and relatives were asking him all kinds of questions. He was bold and uninhibited in telling others of his newfound faith. At times it became rather embarrassing at family gatherings when Dad would get into an argument with the in-laws regarding eternal salvation through faith in Christ. He was asked to teach Sunday school classes in our Mennonite church until the church leadership became alarmed at his teaching.

One evening, the church leaders came to our home and met with Dad in our living room. They questioned Dad about his "religious" experience and about his Sunday school lessons. Dad shared his personal testimony and told them that he knew on the authority of God's Word that he was going to heaven when he died because his eternal salvation was dependent upon the grace and mercy of the Lord Jesus Christ. After much discussion, Dad was informed that his membership in the Mennonite Church was terminated. Some church members shunned Dad and his business while others sought him out to talk about this great salvation Jesus had to offer to all who believed.

A DATE'S INFLUENCE

For that next year after Dad's salvation experience, I watched my Dad's faith in action. I questioned him regarding this "being saved" business. I challenged him on occasion to prove that once we are saved that God would keep us in His fold. I had been taught that one got to heaven by doing good deeds. I assumed that when I died and stood in judgment, God would open His big book, look up my name, and measure my good deeds against my bad deeds. If the good deeds outweighed the bad ones, I would make it into heaven. But, if the reverse were true, I was doomed to hell. I could not intellectually abandon all that I had been taught for seventeen years for some teaching that was an exact contradiction. But I looked. I listened. I learned.

In May of 1949, I graduated from high school and my Mother and Dad made plans to go back to Keswick for another Bible conference. They asked me to join them on the weekend. At the age of eighteen and the proud owner of my new 1949 Pontiac, I decided that I had nothing better to do that weekend so I drove to the New Jersey conference site. I was just an observer and not a seeker for a religious experience. I enjoyed boating on the lake and some of the other activities. On Sunday afternoon, I noticed one of the waitresses. She was cute and I asked her if she wanted to go for a ride in my new Pontiac. She consented and on that beautiful summer Sunday afternoon, we drove around the countryside. At one point I pulled off to the side of the road and we talked.

Imagine my surprise when she had the audacity to begin talking to me about the Lord. She was a relatively new Christian and she began to tell me the same things my Dad had been sharing. She explained that God's gift was eternal life and that He died on the Cross to pay the penalty for my sins so that I could be reconciled to a holy God. To be truthful, I had had other things on my mind when I parked the car, but I listened to my date very intently. She had never met my Dad, yet she spoke the same language. This was not just a coincidence. I was challenged. I realized that although I had done good deeds, taken the church catechism classes and been baptized, somehow that still didn't seem to qualify me for forgiveness and eternal life. I now know the Holy Spirit was working on me and drawing me to Himself.

That very night, I got on my knees and confessed my need to the Lord and invited Him to take over my life. As a result of that date and my Dad's influence, I committed my life to Christ. God found me and I surrendered to Him. I was relieved, and rejoiced to know that my sins were forgiven and that I was starting over with a brand new life.

After praying, I had an assurance that I was truly forgiven and had this gift of eternal life. I told God I would do anything He desired of me if I could just know for certain that I was going to heaven when I died. This truth was confirmed as I read John 5:24—"*He that hears my word and believes on Him that sent me has everlasting life and shall not come into condemnation but is passed from death unto life*" (KJV).

That waitress didn't know of my conversion to Christ that night because I lost contact with her. She wrote me a letter when I got home but before I could answer her, I lost her address. I often said that when I got to heaven, I wanted to look her up and thank her for pointing me to the Savior.

One evening, fifty years later, the telephone rang while I was working on my computer at home. My wife, Jackie, put down her book and answered the phone. A female voice on the other end of the line asked if this was the residence of Dick Snavely and Jackie said "yes." She asked if this was the Dick Snavely who used to live in Lancaster County and Jackie, becoming just a little suspicious, assured her that it was. Then she asked if this Dick Snavely had blue eyes and a dimple. About this time Jackie was becoming alarmed. When the caller identified my round face and thinning hair, Jackie was really suspicious and suggested that the caller had better speak directly to me.

Up until this time, I was hearing primarily just one side of this telephone conversation so I didn't know what to expect. When I picked up the phone, this lady began to tell me that I had dated her many years ago. "Wait just one minute," I said. I knew my memory was not perfect but I would surely remember any girls that I had dated.

At first I thought she was joking. I told her that I did not know her. I denied that I had ever been in her town of Eagles Mere, PA. In fact, I was sure I had never heard of Eagles Mere. I began to feel that I was being set up to be "framed" or something. I knew that I had done nothing to worry about, but thought this lady was trying to pull a fast one.

She said that she heard my voice and name on the radio and thought perhaps I was the Dick Snavely that she had dated. Then she said, "Didn't you have a blue 1949 Pontiac?" I told her that she was correct. That was over fifty years ago and now I began to take her seriously.

After some reminiscing, we discovered that we both attended the Keswick Bible Conference in the summer of 1949. I asked her if she was a waitress at the conference. She confirmed that she had been working as a waitress to earn money for college. Suddenly the lights came on. Could she be the waitress that I took for a ride in my Pontiac that Sunday afternoon? The one who had the courage to talk to me about her faith in Jesus Christ?

That was the only time I had ever spent with her, but I had never forgotten her because of her bold Christian witness to me. For some reason she had never forgotten me either and now, after fifty years, Joan Wright was making contact with me. She had never known that I trusted Christ that night as a result of her witness. I shared with her how her witness brought me to my knees and to Christ that very evening. I explained how it all happened and thanked her for her boldness. She was so grateful and I was glad that I didn't have to wait until I got to heaven to thank her.

TOTAL UNCONDITIONAL SURRENDER

After that Sunday afternoon date in Keswick, NJ I returned home and repeated my life commitment to my Lord. Somehow I knew that God had a plan for my life and that He was going to show it to me. He took the keys of my life and I have been following Him ever since. I prayed a prayer of commitment that day with all of the sincerity that I had. I said, "O Lord, I give up all my own plans and purposes, all my own desires and hopes, and accept Thy will for my life. I give myself, my life, my all utterly to Thee to be Thine forever. Fill me and seal me with Thy Holy Spirit. Use me as Thou wilt; send me where Thou wilt; work out Thy whole will in my life at any cost, now and forever." I still carry this prayer in my wallet to remind myself to regularly renew my commitment to Him. I have not been perfect, but my heart's desire is in this prayer.

After returning home from that weekend in Keswick, my cup was full and running over. My heart was overflowing with gratitude and joy. I felt like a prisoner on death row who had been freed with all charges dropped and my record expunged. I could not thank and praise the Lord enough for what He had done for me. I was bursting at the seams with thankfulness and now I wanted to seal my commitment to follow Jesus Christ.

I was at home alone that evening and found myself paging through an old hymnal. I got my silver trumpet out of its case and I began to play and sing and pray these words: "I'll go where you want me to go dear Lord; I'll do what you want me to do. I'll say what you want me to say dear Lord, I'll be what you want me to be." I played a verse with my trumpet and then I sang the words. I played and sang this song over and over again as my prayer to the Lord with my tears of rejoicing freely flowed down my cheeks. It was all for what He had done for me. There was no one at home to impress, so I was not worried that my playing and singing was not perfect. It was real, and that was enough. I was never more sincere in all of my life. I was communicating with my heavenly Father in whose presence I was made whole. We had a good time.

CHANGES

God had revealed His Truth to me through my Dad, my date, and His Word. "I once was lost but now am found... was blind but now I see." I experienced His Amazing Grace that summer day in 1949 and things have just never been the same. I began to take a long hard look at my life and future. I began memorizing Bible verses. I attended Youth for Christ rallies in Lancaster, PA. I began telling others of this wonderful salvation and gift of forgiveness and eternal life. I now understood my Dad's motivation in memorizing Bible verses and spreading the Gospel. Selfish desires to become a millionaire were gone. Instead of becoming a businessman, I now wanted to become a Christian business-man—and the best one that I could be.

In one day, I became a new person with a new outlook. My focus today is still to do whatever God's plan is for my life. He is my Commander in Chief and I report to Him daily. My motivation comes from the love of Jesus Christ. The Apostle Paul said, *"For Christ's love compels us... "* (II Corinthians 5:14 NIV). I cannot help but tell people about Jesus Christ.

I DID NOT GET GOD—GOD GOT ME. Someone once reminded me that "All of God's people are ordinary people who have been made extraordinary by the purpose He has given them. I'm just an ordinary guy in the hands of an extraordinary God. Unless I have the right purpose intellectually in my mind and lovingly in my heart, I will quickly be diverted from being useful to God. God forbid that that should ever happen. We are not workers for God by choice. Jesus said, *"You did not choose me, but I chose you, and appointed you, that you should go and bear fruit, and that your fruit should remain...*" (John 15:16 NAS).

5

⚜ ⚜

BASIC TRAINING

GOD'S BOOT CAMP

"There is a prepared place for a prepared person."

UP UNTIL THIS TIME, my goal in life had been to become a businessman, to assume Dad's business someday and make lots of money. Now, my goal was to be a Christian businessman and to excel in what I did for His glory. Abe Miller, John Jesburg, and Enos Zimmerman were friends of our family and they suggested that I go to college. College was the farthest thing from my mind. I had a difficult time getting through high school and vowed that I would never pass through the door of another school. They reasoned with me that if I wanted to be the best Christian businessman possible, then attending a Christian college was the answer. They told me that God had a plan for me and that there was a prepared place for a prepared person. I finally agreed this was the direction I should pursue. Since these friends were students at

Bob Jones University, they immediately suggested that I also attend BJU.

I applied to this BJU school, of which I had never heard. I was informed by the University that my references indicated that I had had a lot of trouble with the Pennsylvania State Police. My reckless driving record had caught up with me. After much consideration, they finally agreed to accept me as a student at BJU with probationary status. I had to agree not to haul any passengers in my car at any time during my freshman year. Dr. Bob Jones Sr., the founder, said that if I came to BJU, I would have to learn how to take it on the chin. I accepted his challenge and began making preparations to attend the University in the fall of 1950.

Unfortunately, I did not have the slightest idea of what was involved in attending college. I packed up my Pontiac and headed to Greenville, South Carolina, along with my cousin Sonny Shenk who was a student at the University and my self-appointed navigator. When we arrived, it was raining and it continued raining for several days. Being a relatively new campus, there was red mud everywhere. I discovered that I had four roommates who would share my small room. One was a musical loony tune who would set jars of water on the window sill and tap out different tunes. It was the first time I was away from home for an extended period of time. Boy, was I ever discouraged.

Then it came time to register for classes. It appeared to me that one needed a college education just to work through the registration process. I was confounded with the stacks of papers indicating the available courses along with forms to be filled out. What in the world was Shakespeare 201 or Greek 100A? I was so discouraged at the process that I was ready to go back home, but Sonny Shenk offered to help me. I told him that all I was interested in was taking some Bible courses since I wanted to be a Christian businessman with some good Bible knowledge.

When I received my schedule and started classes, I suddenly discovered that Sonny had signed me up for the ministerial course. My first class was *Elementary Greek* followed by *The Preacher and His Problems*. I was stunned and didn't know what to do except to attend these classes. I have often said that I was never "called" into the ministry but rather was "pushed." God had a plan.

During my first month on the BJU campus, I was involved in Christian service activities, which included giving my testimony to inmates in local jails. After several months of this Christian service, I began to question if the business world was really God's plan for me. I had this strong desire to tell people the truth about God's plan of salvation, especially young people. After much soul searching and remembering my prayer of commitment, I told the Lord that I would forget the business world and give 100% of my time to ministry, if that was His plan. God gave me real peace about that decision. Now I just had to tell Dad.

Dad was a little disappointed at first when I told him that I was no longer interested in the business and wanted to spend the rest of my life reaching people for Christ. He was also slightly envious of me because of his own desire to be in the ministry full-time.

My college days were some of the best years of my life, although life as a student at Bob Jones University was very different than anything I had experienced up until that point. I appreciated the discipline and accountability that was required at the University. I learned the importance of keeping commitments, being on time for appointments and having a positive attitude. On the inside of every door in the dormitory was a sign which said, "Griping not tolerated. Constructive criticism appreciated."

Christian service was encouraged for all students but especially for those in the ministerial class. Most of my weekends were involved with ministry to prisoners in the local jails. I led a group of "preacher boys" to the Spartanburg jail every Sunday afternoon where we witnessed, passed out Gospel tracts and preached. Many times we were put in the cells with the prisoners. God took me out of my comfort zone numerous times as the jail door clanged behind me and the guard disappeared down stairs, leaving nothing between me and the prisoners but my Bible.

I also conducted a Sunday school class for the Spartanburg City firemen on Sunday mornings. My first Sunday in that role brought me an unforgettable experience. We were meeting on the second floor of the fire house when suddenly the fire siren began whining in the middle of my lesson. All of a sudden the whole class got up, slid down the fire pole to the ground floor, jumped on the fire trucks and was gone. I was left alone with my lesson as my class disappeared.

Attendance at all meals was another requirement at BJU. This helped students to develop social skills and to make new friends. We learned how to seat a lady by pulling out a chair for her and assisting her up to the table, how to receive a dish of food with the right hand and pass it with the left hand, and how to wait for the hostess to place her fork on her plate before beginning to eat. It was good training in etiquette and helped to equip me in my Christian life. Good manners and social skills are refinements that make a man a positive witness for Christ.

Living with five students in one room during my freshman year guaranteed that part of my education included learning to live and cooperate with other people. During my second year I only had three other roommates. Our room consisted of four bunk beds, a wash bowl, mirror, desk, chairs, two dressers and a place to hang clothes. Four students living in a very small room required a lot of give and take.

When that wake-up bell sounded at 6:30 every morning, we had to have both feet on the floor before the monitor checked our room. Beds had to be made, shoes placed neatly under the beds, waste cans emptied, sink and mirror cleaned and everything in order. Each of us had assigned chores that had to be completed before going to breakfast. If the hall monitor found something out of place, the person responsible for that area would have to face the discipline committee the following week. If found guilty, he received a demerit on his school record.

Demerits were handed out for nearly everything including being late for class or a meal, failing to wear a coat and tie to supper, or for making noise after the 10:30 lights-out at night. Skipping a class drew 25 demerits. A student was expelled if he acquired 150 demerits during the semester. This happened quite often, especially during the early weeks of a new semester when new students arrived. It was real discipline for me but it was exactly what I needed. God was preparing me for a prepared place where discipline was needed.

Since I had been accepted at BJU on a probationary basis, I was very careful about how I behaved. I wanted to make a good record for myself, but it really required a considerable adjustment. My first demerit came one evening after the lights-out bell sounded and everything and everyone was quiet. My roommate threw something at my bed and I threw the remainder of an apple that I had just consumed back at him. That apple core bounced off his bed, out into the hall and fell at the feet of the floor monitor who was in the process of checking rooms. The monitor came into our room and began questioning each of us. I was literally shaking as he worked over each student. As he approached my bed, I knew I had to tell the truth and I confessed to the misdeed before he had time to finish his first question. That next week I appeared before the discipline committee to plead my case. Guilty was the verdict and my first demerit was recorded. I was consoled by the knowledge that this demerit would not count on my permanent record as long as I received no more than five by the end of the semester.

Despite my poor conduct before my college days and being accepted at the University on probation, I was able to complete four years at Bob Jones University without one demerit on my permanent record. I shall always be grateful for the rules and regulations that were very strictly enforced. I was never a perfect angel but I was determined to do my best and set a good record, especially since I was now a real Christian and on my way to heaven because of God's wonderful grace and pardon.

One of my favorite times of the day was Chapel, when Dr. Bob Jones, Sr. would share his heart with us. He referred to us as his boys and girls. He was a compassionate fighter for the Truth. He would preach on some of his famous topics, such as "The test of your character is what it takes to stop you." We could always expect that sermon to come at the beginning of the school year when so many new freshmen were overwhelmed with college pressures and being away from home. He would encourage us all not to quit because quitting was the easiest thing to do. Another favorite saying was "The door to success swings on the hinges of opposition." In other words, if you are going to be successful, you must be prepared for opposition somewhere along the way. Other famous Jonesisms included, "The greatest ability is dependability," and "Your reputation is what people think you are, but your character is what God knows you are." Every week he drove these truths home to my heart and motivated our "preacher boy" class of 1,000 to win souls for Jesus.

While at Bob Jones University, I met a man who would later become a very important force in my life. His name was Dick Coons and he was a year or two ahead of me in school. He was a funny guy of about 5'7" and sported the mandatory short haircut of the University. You could always tell when one of his jokes or tricks was coming by the silly grin that would crease across his face. Dick had a take-charge type personality and was host of the dining room table to which I was assigned for one three-week period. As an upperclassman, Dick was expected to set an example to the newer students regarding table manners and social skills. Over those three weeks, we developed a relationship as we met three times a day for our meals. Dick Coons graduated from the University and, unbeknown to me, went on to become the director of Rochester Youth for Christ.

MORE TRAINING—ALASKA

I joined the mission prayer band, a group of students who met every week to pray for missionaries around the world. Two other classmates, LeRoy and Sam joined me in praying for missionaries in Alaska, and we got the bright idea to spend the next summer witnessing and preaching the Gospel in Alaska. When we began to raise money for the trip, Dad announced that we needed an older person to accompany us. I believe Dad really wanted to go along more to witness than to supervise, although we were very glad that he joined us. He wound up being the "glue" that held us together.

Dad bought a Chevrolet Carry-All for the trip. We loaded it down with cases of baked beans, soups, and the like. We set up evangelistic meetings in churches of friends from Pennsylvania to Montana where we would preach and provide music. The University required that all music had to be pre-approved for such evangelistic meetings. Our music was my trumpet, and I had only four numbers approved. At one church, we had five meetings. LeRoy and Sam requested that I repeat one of the numbers so we could honestly say that I was repeating one of the songs by special request.

As we drove up the graveled and dusty Alaskan highway, we suffered many flat tires and broken headlights. We had no motels, but slept on park benches and tables. We would lie in our sleeping bags, wide-eyed, listening to wild animals and strange sounds in the night. One morning LeRoy tried to put his shoe on but couldn't get his foot in the whole way. He jumped as a mouse followed his foot out of that shoe.

We explored the beauty of God's creation that summer while we conducted evangelistic services in Anchorage, Fairbanks, and many remote villages. We worked with several missionaries and even helped to construct a mission hospital in Glen Allen. At the end of summer, we had to rush home to begin classes at the University. We drove straight through for six days from Anchorage, Alaska to Lancaster, Pennsylvania. For all six nights, we slept on top of our equipment in that old Chevy Carry-All truck. We had a real vibrating bed as we bounced along for thousands of miles on the hard and uneven boxes. All four of us took turns driving while the others would sleep. We did not stop except to fix flat tires and buy gasoline. Gasoline stations on the Alaskan highway were few and far between, so we would fill up every time we came to one. When we stopped for gas we would put cans of beans and soup on the engine manifold and the next time we stopped, our meal would be heated and ready to eat. It was quite an experience.

It was so delightful to arrive home and sleep in a real bed, but almost immediately I had to travel back to South Carolina to begin my next semester at BJU. It was very difficult saying goodbye to my sweetheart, Jackie, after being away all summer and then seeing her for only half a day before leaving again. In spite of our separation, our relationship was growing deeper all the time. Absence really did make the heart grow fonder. She was extra special to me. I couldn't wait until we could be together for the rest of our lives. Little did I know then how important she would be in the future work to which God called us.

6

∽ ∾

THE ONE AND ONLY

A GIFT OF GREAT VALUE

> "A gift of great value from God. She brings
> honor to her husband."
> Proverbs 18:22 KJV

FOR MOST OF MY TEEN years, girls were a distant second in my life. They were important, but not nearly as important as my pride and joy—my '49 Pontiac. When I committed my life to Christ, the Pontiac became a distant second to Jesus Christ. Even though girls now ranked third, they were quickly climbing the charts. I was embarrassed around girls because I had a bad case of acne during my teen years. Dad took me to a skin specialist for treatments, but they didn't help. I brushed my face hard with a vegetable brush and soap, but to no avail. My face would turn fire engine red and nearly bleed from the scrubbing. I would then put facial cream on for healing. It hurt, but inside I was hurting more because I thought everyone looked at my face with repulsion. Because of my pizza face complexion, I did not feel accepted by girls, and so my car got most of my attention.

Little did I realize that perhaps God allowed this unsightly complexion to keep this guy from becoming a proud obnoxious kid. It certainly was a humbling experience and one from which I could not escape. It kept me in check with the opposite sex.

One of the first approaches I ever made for a date was a disaster. The girl lived out in the country in an area called Weaverland. She was a nice looking Mennonite girl with wavy hair and a nice smile. I drove by her house a couple of times and waited until it was dusk before finally parking my car a short distance from the front of her house. I didn't want anyone to see me in case I changed my mind. When it was nearly dark, I nervously stepped from my car. My hands were sweaty. My heart was thumping. I mustered my courage and I finally knocked on the door. I waited for what seemed like a million years.

I looked through the large glass window in the front door and I saw her coming down the steps toward me. I panicked. My tongue stuck to the roof of my mouth as if I had a mouth full of peanut butter. I had no idea what I was going to say. As she approached the door, I ran off the porch and hid behind a large evergreen tree. She turned on the porch light, opened the door, and looked around. She waited. I was sure she heard my heart pounding behind that tree next to the porch. I feared she would take a few steps to get a better look. I knew I was a dead duck if she did because she would have been face to face with me. When she didn't see anyone, she finally closed the door and turned off the light. I broke out into a sweat and was ready for an extra supply of oxygen as my breathing became laborious. After taking a few moments to compose myself, I ran to my car. Then I drove away from her house without my headlights and with my heart still thumping. I never did get a date with that beautiful girl.

One day a Christian friend suggested that I ought to give my date life to God and start praying for a wife. This was really something new. Pray for a wife? No way! That was one decision that I could make for myself. I did not want God's help with that decision because I was afraid that He might give me some old "hag" for a wife. I had my own ideas and expectations of what she should look and be like. Obviously, my concept of God needed some work. Then, one day I read the verse *"Delight thyself also in the Lord: and He shall give thee the desires of thine heart"* (Psalm 37:4 KJV). Wow! I couldn't believe my eyes. I thought, "Is that what it really says? Is this one of God's promises?" I read this verse over many times and began to realize that if I did my part of "delighting myself in Him" then He promised to give to me the desires of my heart. I get to do the "delighting" and He does the "giving." And He doesn't give just any old thing; He gives the desires of *my* heart.

I memorized and meditated on this promise for many days. I began to do everything I could to "delight myself in Him" and I began praying for His choice for a wife. What a big step of faith for me. Could I really trust God to give me the wife of all wives? Out of the entire universe could He bring that woman into my life that would be the desire of my heart? Slowly, I began to realize that God already knew the woman that would be the perfect match for me, not only now but fifty or sixty years after the honeymoon. I figured if I could trust God for my destiny, then I could trust Him for the right life partner. It took me a while to come to this conclusion, but I had determined to trust God.

THE SET-UP

My cousin, Molly Weaver, invited me to a birthday party at her home in Strasburg one Saturday evening. The house was full of couples, but I was dateless. I didn't have a girlfriend at the time, so I was on the prowl. Then I saw this beautiful blue-eyed girl. She had high cheek bones, wavy hair and the small Mennonite covering on her head. She was slim, attractive and neatly dressed. When Molly introduced me to her, I was nearly speechless. Her name was Jacqueline DeVere. At first appearance, she looked like she might fit "the desire of my heart," but she had a date that night so she was not available. I dismissed my chances of ever dating her because she was far above my class. Little did I realize all of the help I was receiving from my cousin Molly. She and Jackie attended the same school and Molly continued to tell Jackie that I was a nice guy and she should date me sometime.

I guess Molly knew that I would never have the courage to ask Jackie for a date, so after many months had gone by she decided to take matters into her own hands. One summer Sunday evening, after service at the Strasburg Mennonite Church, a group of my friends were standing outside of the church talking "guy talk" while admiring a nearby group of girls who were probably talking "girl talk." One of my buddies and Molly's boyfriend, Earl Clark, came up to me and informed me that he had made arrangements with Jackie DeVere for me to take her home and that I was not to leave without her. I was flabbergasted. I thought it was a joke. I couldn't believe he would do something like this—forcing my hand.

I waited until almost all of the girls were gone to approach Jackie, who was still talking with Dot Mellinger, one of her girl friends. My friend Bob Musser was traveling with me that evening and he had "eyes" for Dot. I asked Jackie if Earl Clark had really spoken to her about me taking her home. She said "yes," but quickly informed me in no uncertain terms that I would have to follow her to her house since she had driven the old 1935 Ford sedan to church that evening.

I was overjoyed! This was an opportunity to date a girl with whom I never thought I would have a chance. Bob and I happily followed the girls to Jackie's house a few miles away in West Lampeter. Our first date was a lot of fun. Jackie had just celebrated her nineteenth birthday and we talked and laughed about many things. We had a great evening together and I really liked her but I was not certain how she felt about me, old pizza face. I decided to take a bold step and ask her for another date. She informed me that she had another commitment for that day. I began to melt, but her answer had sounded like a legitimate excuse and not a rejection, so in fear and trembling of another humiliation, I tried for another day. To my amazement, she agreed and we began to date on a regular basis. Bob and Dottie continued to date also, and eventually married.

Jackie is the third of five children. She was born in Lancaster but her family moved to Detroit, where her dad worked in a factory. He was an alcoholic and spent most of his weekly paycheck on booze, causing his family to live in poverty. Often Jackie and her siblings would search garbage cans for food. Many nights they would sleep on newspapers with old coats. They always looked forward to receiving Thanksgiving dinners from a settlement house in Detroit. Zollar's Gospel Tabernacle offered to provide the family with milk if Jackie and her siblings would attend Sunday school every week. That was where Jackie first heard the Gospel.

Jackie's dad, Jacque DeVere, was a French Canadian. He was forty-four years old when he died of hemorrhaging from his nose. After his death, Jackie's mother moved back to Lancaster and placed Jackie, her brother Clifford, and two sisters, Charlotte and Shirley, in the Millersville Mennonite Children's home. The oldest sister remained with her mother while the mother developed a live-in relationship with her sister's husband.

Jackie was ten years old when she was left in the orphanage and lived there for several years before being placed on the farm of John and Ida Witmer in West Lampeter, PA. There she worked as a farmhand and performed many of the chores such as milking the cows, working in the peach and apple orchards, carrying fire wood, and feeding the livestock. I began dating her while she lived in this old farmhouse. The house lacked many of the modern conveniences such as a bathroom and central heat. A stovepipe ran up through the parlor to the Witmer's bedroom on the second floor. That old stovepipe was the vehicle of communicating many messages to me. If I had not ended our dates by the time midnight rolled around, the taps on that stovepipe from the Witmer's bedroom reminded me that it was time for me to leave.

Upon graduation from West Lampeter High School, Jackie answered an ad and was hired in a doctor's office. She was excited because the money she would earn would enable her to buy her own clothes and have some freedom. However, her foster parents forbid her to leave the farm because they needed her free labor. Jackie was crushed and cried her eyes out the night she had to inform the doctor that she could not take the job. I know the Lord heard her because my cousin Molly once again came into the picture. Molly had a tender heart and was concerned for Jackie. She suggested that Jackie should come and live with her family in Strasburg. Molly's parents, my Uncle Roy and Aunt Betty Weaver kindly opened their home. Jackie shared their home on South Jackson Street in Strasburg with Molly, her sister Peggy, and brother Kenny for about two years. In the meantime, she worked at Clark's potato warehouse and then at the Hamilton Watch factory in Lancaster where she put jewels in watches. The Lord always provides in unusual ways through His people. There must be a special reward for people like Uncle Roy and Aunt Betty who provided for a needy teenager like Jackie.

Jackie had very little as a child and I noticed that she was always very appreciative of everything I did for her. On Valentine's Day I bought her a box of chocolate candy. She was so grateful and said that no one had ever given her a box of candy. On Easter I gave her a flowering plant which she cherished and told all of her friends about. She was excited and always so grateful for the Sunday afternoon trips we would make just riding around the countryside.

I admired her for her character and began to see that she was not only a beautiful person on the outside but had great inner beauty. This lady had high standards and stood up for what she believed. She was not afraid to voice her opinion. It wasn't long before I was convinced that she was God's choice for my lifetime partner. And I was totally in agreement with God's choice. That promise in Psalm 37:4 was becoming reality with me. Now I knew that God would have to convince her that I was His choice for her. I was willing to wait as long as it was necessary.

When I first told her that I loved her, she became very emotional because no one had ever said that to her before. I knew it was not going to be hard to love this woman the rest of my life. It didn't take too long for her to be convinced that I was God's choice for her. We were beginning to love each other more as each day rolled by. I was emotionally depressed when it was time for me to leave her for my first year at Bob Jones University. It was so hard to leave her knowing that it would be over three months before I would see her again. I gave her a big hug and kiss and promised to write her every day. We both shed some tears as I drove off in my Pontiac for the trip south. We wrote letters, but no phone calls were possible, since I was so far away from home in South Carolina. I was only able to come home at Christmas time during the school year.

I cherished her letters. I would check my post office box several times a day, and upon receiving one, I would first smell it before opening it. It always had that perfume smell that reminded me of my future wife. Her letters always consisted of a little bit of news, followed by words that fed my ego. I sensed a little of how God was working in her life as she related experiences of answered prayer and some character building encounters.

My parents really loved Jackie and they decided to surprise me by bringing her to South Carolina for a visit during the Thanksgiving season. They made reservations at the Catalina

Motel just down the road from the University. I was able to get permission to leave the campus with my parents, so Jackie and I were able to spend some valuable time together. Since we were off campus and chaperoned, Jackie and I were allowed to hold hands. Wheeee! Holding hands on campus was not allowed, so this was a thrill. We talked about our lives, plans for the future, and how God was working in our lives. After giving her a kiss, I finally got up the courage to ask her to marry me. Wow! She said "yes," and without any hesitation. My mother and dad were very happy for us. In fact, Dad was always on Jackie's side on almost any issue. He knew that she would be good for his son.

We did not publicly announce our engagement until Christmastime, when the Snavely clan of uncles, aunts, cousins, and grandma were gathered at Uncle Paul and Aunt Blanche Meck's farmhouse. Aunt Blanche, my Dad's sister, always put on a fantastic meal with many different dishes including homemade pies and ice cream. On this occasion she made a cake and before serving it she informed everyone seated around the very long table that inside one piece of the cake was a paper with an important announcement. Whoever found that announcement was to read it aloud. It was not long before someone stood up and read—"This is to announce the engagement of Jackie DeVere to Dick Snavely." Everybody applauded and expressed their congratulations and best wishes. Since engagement rings were not approved by our Mennonite church, I presented Jackie with a cedar chest when I came home for Christmas that year. I may not have given her a diamond, but I knew I had found a real jewel.

My Dad was so impressed with Jackie that he paid her room, board and tuition to Bob Jones University for two semesters. Jackie attended the University during the second semester of my first year and the second semester of my second year. It was great to be together, but difficult because we were not allowed to even hold hands. We did get a thrill out of playing footsie, though, during the Sunday afternoon vesper programs when the lights would be turned down in the auditorium. We often frequented the dating parlor, which at first glance looked like a large furniture showroom. Chairs, floor lamps, end tables, and footstools were everywhere. Couples sat on the comfortable furniture and gazed at each other, rolled their eyes, and chatted. Monitors were carefully watching to be sure there was no touching. During these years, God was preparing both of us for each other. Our relationship transcended the physical. The "no holding hands policy" allowed the spiritual relationship to flourish. I felt that I had obtained favor from the Lord as I read Proverbs 18:22, *"Whoso findeth a wife findeth a good thing, and obtaineth favor from the Lord"* (KJV).

THE MARRIAGE

Coming from a broken home with an alcoholic father, Jackie had always wanted to marry a preacher because she thought that would assure her of a husband who did not drink or smoke. She began making her plans to marry this preacher during the second semester at BJU. Since her father was deceased and she had not seen nor heard from her mother since she was ten, she had to rely on my parents and the Weavers for marriage preparations. Most of the wedding expenses were paid by my father and mother along with my Uncle Roy and Aunt Betty Weaver. Jackie was able to earn enough money working at the Hamilton Watch factory to buy her wedding gown and a few other things for the special day.

We asked our pastor, Dr. Frank C. Torrey of Calvary Church in Lancaster, to perform the ceremony and on June 21, 1952 we were married in the house my parents were renting in Blue Ball, PA. Cousin Molly Weaver Clark played the piano in our living room while the bride and her bridal party of two descended the stairs. It was a very simple ceremony but very meaningful to us both. The ceremony could have been disrupted if my brother Glenn, always the clown, had not discovered Jackie's wedding band which he had dropped on the floor earlier.

My dad was our nervous photographer who enjoyed running around taking pictures of all of the action. We thought that was wonderful, until after the ceremony and reception, when Dad found his camera lens lying on the floor of the front porch. He had taken all of those pictures without a lens in his camera. That's why we have very few wedding pictures. Fortunately, we had arranged for a professional portrait to be taken by a photographer in Lancaster. During the trip to the studio into Lancaster, I had a real moment of concern. Jackie and I were sitting in the back seat while the best man drove my Pontiac. We were in a very joyous mood and celebrating with hugs and kisses until all of a sudden she looked me straight in the eye, grabbed my arm with a tight clench and said, "I got you now." I looked at her and knew that she was dead serious. I began to wonder if I had missed something in all of our courtship. Then she explained that now no other girl could get me since the wedding was over. What a relief.

After the wedding we headed to Niagara Falls for our honeymoon with $80 in my pocket. Our first motel room cost five dollars and gasoline cost fifteen cents a gallon. Our largest expense was for a guided tour of Niagara Falls. We spent a lot of personal time together, ate very little, and lived on love. I knew people could tell we were newlyweds because we had a twinkle in our eyes and grins on our faces all of the time. We were two lovebirds enjoying every minute of it. We honeymooned until we ran out of money after one week and then headed home.

After the honeymoon, life went on. We lived at my parents house until school resumed in the fall, then I packed my bags and, with my bride, headed to South Carolina to begin my junior year at the University as a married student. Jackie and I were both twenty-one years old when we got married. On her 21st

birthday, Jackie had received a Social Security check for eight hundred dollars which had accumulated since her father's death. We used that money to buy a used World War II house trailer to live in near the University campus. It was 8' x 30' with Masonite sides, metal roof, and no bath. It was parked in a trailer court, across from the side entrance to the University. Since very few trailers had bathrooms, we all used common bathrooms and showers which were housed in an expanded trailer. It was located next to our lot, and its odors seeped through our bedroom window all hours of the day and night.

Our furniture consisted of used orange crates covered with towels. I'll never forget sitting down for our first supper of Cheerios and looking across the meager table at my wife whose cooking experience was limited to boiling water. Suddenly it really hit me… I had a new and awesome responsibility as a husband… many responsibilities. Why didn't somebody tell me about this? I was responsible for this woman and her well-being. My paycheck was no longer mine—it was ours. I was the provider and the spiritual head of this new home. So much for the premarital counseling—there was none. For some reason, these added responsibilities never really sank in while we were living at home those two months after the wedding with Mother and Dad picking up all of the expenses. All of a sudden reality set in. Wow!

Little by little, God gave me strength to rise to the occasion. There were numerous adjustments that these two lovebirds had to make that no one had ever warned us about. It was one of God's refining processes which are necessary for life and service. I believe it is called maturing. Things were no longer "mine" or "hers," but rather "ours."

Jackie went to work in a garment factory in Greenville to help put food on the table. We agreed that she would work for the last two years of my schooling and that we wouldn't have any children until I graduated because of our financial situation. God had other plans. Jackie began having morning sickness. I told her it was just in her head because of new surroundings and responsibilities. If my dear, sweet bride were capable of murder, I would have been dead for even making such a suggestion. Then we discovered that she was pregnant and could no longer work. This called for an adjustment for which I was unprepared. Certainly God must have had a plan in all of this.

I began working at night in a garment factory while carrying a full load of classes during the day. I, along with several other university students, laid rolls of material on long tables for the garment workers to cut out the next morning. The pay was seventy cents an hour, but it put food on the table. The Lord provided in many ways for those last two years of college. We daily claimed the verse in Philippians 4:19—*"My God shall supply all your need according to his riches in glory by Christ Jesus"* (KJV).

One evening I noticed there was not very much food on the table. We discussed what we would eat for breakfast the next morning since our wallets were empty and the food shelves were bare, except for some staples. We really were not too worried because we knew we were in God's will. We knew that God had a plan and would provide for us. God often gave us a peace that is not of this world. Later that evening we went for a drive and upon our return to the house trailer, there was such a large stack of food piled up in front of our door that we could not get into the trailer until we moved it. There were boxes of cereal, fruit, milk, cans of vegetables, bread, and even snacks. There must have been over forty dollars worth of groceries stacked there. God made a delivery through His people. It was a great lesson in faith that has impacted our lives to this very day.

Being a college student, husband, father, and breadwinner was a real challenge. Studies never came easily, but I did finally make it to the Dean's List one semester. Also, out of our ministerial class of one thousand men, I was one of seven students who made it to the semi-finals in the annual preacher boy contest with my sermon on faith. At the conclusion of my senior year, I was ordained to the ministry by the Gospel Fellowship Association, which was a separate organization from the University but administered by BJU leaders.

Ten months into the marriage, our first child, Carol Ann, was born. Fourteen months later, and just two months after graduation, our second child, Rick, was born. In just two short years I had become a husband, a father of two children, and a University graduate. I was not ready for fatherhood. I was still learning to be a husband and spiritual leader of my new home. Once again, the reality of my responsibility began to sink in deeper. But God had plans and I was on my way to becoming a godly man.

God's plan for my life would never have been complete without including my wife Jackie. She has been a tremendous help-meet and mother. She shared my vision for this ministry. She encouraged me when I was down and lovingly brought me down when I was getting too proud. Often she would tell me that she was very proud of me. She was always careful to make me look good in public. As a mother and wife, she always put me and the kids ahead of herself. When money was short, she spent what we had for clothes for the children or me before buying clothes for herself. When our tight budget allowed for either a new suit for me or a new dress for her, she demanded that I get the new suit. She spent valuable time with the children as they were growing up and always had great times discussing school when they came home. Our kids loved our home because she made it a refuge for them. Without Jackie, I could never have enjoyed any successes in life nor been the leader of this ministry that God brought into existence. God had a plan for my life and Jackie was certainly an integral part of that plan.

7

⁊ ⁊

PAINFUL PREPARATION

WHERE DO I GO FROM HERE, GOD?

"Trust in the Lord with all thy heart; and lean not unto thine own
understanding. In all thy ways acknowledge Him
and He shall direct thy paths."
Proverbs 3:5-6 KJV

MY FUTURE WAS VERY uncertain. I had just graduated from University and would soon have my second child, but I had no job. The head of our BJU ministerial class, Dr. Gilbert Stenholm, suggested that I consider a ministry with Youth for Christ. I contemplated it, but never followed up on his suggestion until some time later.

My Dad was still operating the business, but was really spending much of his time on the road running the big Eastman Kodak arc movie projector in stadiums and arenas for the Billy Graham Evangelistic Film Association. He encouraged me to apply for a job with the Billy Graham organization. I traveled to

Washington, DC for my interview with Mr. Walt Smith. I was hired and I began my first full-time job in a Christian ministry.

I was a film evangelist. It was my responsibility to set up and personally conduct showings of the Billy Graham Evangelistic films. I contacted pastors, scheduled bookings in churches, showed the film and gave the invitation after Billy Graham's message. On some occasions I scheduled, organized and directed city-wide film showings where I worked with ministerial groups and Christian businessmen's organizations that sponsored the events. I worked with their committees on promotion, finances, counseling, parking, lighting, ushers, etc. My territory was Virginia, West Virginia, Maryland, and Delaware. I worked with hundreds of pastors and laymen from many different denominations in these four states. It was a great learning experience. This broadened my perspective and gave me an interdenominational outlook.

After nearly two years of traveling with my movie projector, I grew weary of being away from my family. There were times that I would break down and weep while driving away from my family for another week or two on the road. At the same time, I was not aware that my absence from home was taking its toll on my wife. She had difficulty sleeping at night. Her appetite was gone. She never complained, but when I learned that her weight had dropped below 100 pounds, I knew something was wrong and decided that she needed to see a doctor. When her doctor suggested that her weight loss was probably connected to my absence, I thought it was probably time for a change. When my son Rickie called our milkman "daddy," I knew it was time for a change. I was torn between ministry and family. I felt guilty resigning from the evangelistic film ministry and yet I felt responsible for my wife and children. Through these experiences, the Lord impressed upon me that my responsibility was to my family first and then to ministry. This has been my desire all of my life, even though I may have slipped at times.

Once I resigned, I asked the Lord for the opportunity to pastor a church. I thought I knew what I needed. I thought I knew what God's plan was for my life at this stage. Here I was telling God what I wanted and not listening to what He wanted. He gave me what I asked for. He not only gave me a new opportunity, but He took me through some interesting experiences which I later recognized as preparation. Little did I realize at the time just how much work in me He was going to do.

THE WEST VIRGINIA EXPERIENCE

After concluding one of my final evangelistic film showings with the Billy Graham ministry, I had to travel through the mountains of West Virginia to get home. All of a sudden, in the darkness of night, I came upon an unlighted sign that said "Road Out." About fifty feet ahead there was a small blinking orange light on a trestle where one-half of the road had collapsed down over the mountain side. I was alarmed that there was such little warning for such a dangerous situation. At the time I said to myself, "I would never want to live in a place like this." The place was McConnell, West Virginia.

Shortly thereafter, in answer to my prayer for a pastorate, I received an invitation to candidate for a small church. Guess where that church was. That's right—it was in McConnell, West Virginia. It was a little non-denominational church located in the coal fields of Logan County. All that I knew about the church was that they wanted a Bob Jones University graduate as their pastor. I thought that must be a good sign. After candidating, the church called me as their pastor. I was frightened at the thought of preparing three sermons a week plus performing all of the other duties of a faithful pastor. Again, I was reminded of Dr. Bob, Sr. saying that God will never put you in a place without giving you everything that you need to glorify the Lord in that place. Armed with that thought and confidence in the Lord, I eagerly moved ahead with my new challenge. All of a sudden, God gave me a desire for the place about which I had once said, "I would never want to live here." The reason for the change of heart I believe was my desire to be where the Lord wanted me to be.

We moved into the parsonage, which was across the street from the Tabernacle. The Tabernacle was a one story building with several Sunday school classrooms. It was not an attractive building. It had a dingy brown asphalt shingle siding. Immediately behind the building was the river. It seemed like all of these small coal mining towns had mountains on two sides, a river, and a railroad track. The mountains were so steep, I was told, that the residents planted their gardens with shot guns— shooting seeds into the side of the hills. One guy claimed to have broken his leg when he fell out of his garden.

Jackie had to be careful when she hung the wash out to dry because when the train came through town it would blow coal soot all over the clean clothing. My Dad, concerned about Jackie being great with child at this time, bought her a clothes dryer to save her laundry.

The services of this little church in the coal fields of West Virginia included Wednesday evening prayer meetings and a Sunday evening service but no Sunday morning worship services. I soon discovered that they had no doctrinal statement, by-laws or constitution. The membership consisted of many doctrinal persuasions such as Methodists, Presbyterians and some Pentecostals. The congregation was comprised of school teachers, businessmen, coal miners, and laborers, but they were not very literate on the teachings of God's Word. In one of my first services I noticed a man and woman sitting in the second row of pews. The lady had decay holes in her front teeth. During my preaching, she would suck air through those holes, throw her hands in the air, and yell, "Bless him, Jesus!" The man just sat there. I later discovered that they were married, but not to each other. I knew that I had a job before me.

Mr. M. was the chairman of the deacon board. He was a foreman in a coal mine, a man in his forties who seldom smiled. He ran the church. The other power in the church was the man who owned the organ, Mr. D. His wife was the only one allowed to play this instrument unless permission was granted by Mr. D.'s family.

I successfully prepared a constitution and by-laws for the church body to adopt. Where we ran into difficulty was with my new doctrinal statement because Mr. M. believed in baptismal regeneration. He held to the belief that one had to be baptized for the remission of his sins. This is not true since the Bible teaches in Ephesians 2:8-9 that man is *"saved by grace through faith and not of ourselves because it is a gift of God and not of works."* After much debate and discussion by the church board, my doctrinal statement was approved. Mr. M., as the chairman of the board, however, never brought the doctrinal statement to a church vote.

During the board's discussion over the doctrinal statement, I suggested that we begin a Sunday morning worship service where we could teach the doctrines of the Bible. The church board finally agreed to begin a morning worship service. These services generated much interest as we began teaching the book of Galatians. God began to work in hearts and some people trusted Christ as their Savior.

I conducted the choir, led singing, ran the youth group, directed the Easter Cantata, and preached. It was also my responsibility to visit new people who moved into town and those who were ill. I made a map of the whole community with each house marked indicating the number of people living in each house. In my youthful zeal, I was prepared to reach that whole community for Christ.

One day, I knocked on the door of a house in town. When a man came to the door, I introduced myself to him and extended an invitation for him and his wife to come to church. He stunned me by saying that he had just buried his wife the day before. I extended my sympathies and he invited me into his home. He told me the story of how he and his wife had worked hard all of their lives and how they had just purchased this house when his wife came down with cancer and died. He said, "We were just ready to live." I asked him if he was ready to die, and explained that one is never ready to live until they are ready to die. It was a great opportunity to share the Gospel with this man as he grieved.

We were reaching new people. Even though many were yet unsaved, people were excited about what was happening in the church. Several young people trusted Christ as Savior. But change did not make Mr. M., the chairman of the deacon board, comfortable.

After about five months of pastoring, Mr. M. made a surprise announcement in the morning service that there would be a vote of confidence on the pastor that evening. It was a shock to everyone, but since the chairman had never brought the by-laws, constitution and doctrinal statement to the church for a vote, he could still run the church as he desired.

I was confused. I thought I had been faithful in my pastoral duties. I was reaching out to the community. Souls were being saved. We had an effective ministry with the young people, but many were not yet saved. I still had work to do.

I knew there were a handful of adult members who did not like me because they said that I was not a preacher but rather a teacher, but they seemed to be in the minority. One evening they took me to a service in another local church. The preacher spent most of the time pacing up and down the aisle, bellowing and pointing his finger at people. He yelled about going to hell and called for repentance. It was quite an experience, but they told me that *that* was preaching. Right then and there I knew I was not the preacher this group wanted. I felt like there were two forces at work struggling for the hearts and minds of these people. The mental stress became almost unbearable, but I determined that I would not quit. Quitting would grant Satan a victory.

The Sunday evening of the confidence vote, I preached what I thought would be my last sermon at that church. In my youthful ambitious and inexperienced way, I preached my heart out and told the people to vote carefully, because if I were to continue pastoring that church, I would boldly preach Christ and Him crucified, risen and coming again. I proclaimed that salvation was by grace through faith in Christ and not of works. It was straightforward. I was determined that I would not quit as long as I received a majority vote, regardless how difficult and stressful it would be. I was very doubtful that anyone would vote for me after such a sermon. I asked the young people not to vote if they were not Christians.

After the sermon the people voted. The congregation sat in silence while the board members counted the votes in the Sunday school room. Everybody was anxiously awaiting the results. I sat by myself in the front row, with thoughts of moving on my mind. It seemed like an eternity before there was any stirring in that Sunday school room. It seemed like they had enough time to count the votes three times. Sure enough, they did count them three times. It was that close. Finally Mr. M. stood before the congregation while every person leaned forward to hear his results. He announced that they had counted and recounted and each time it had ended up in a tie vote. There were all kinds of sighs among the congregation. What a shock! I was dumbfounded. I decided that evidently God was not yet finished with me in West Virginia and I was prepared to march ahead for Christ and the church.

Later that night, I saw the board chairman heading toward the parsonage. I didn't know what to think, but I was pretty sure he was not coming to congratulate me. I didn't know how I was going to handle him. When I answered the door he had an ugly look on his face and said, "You're lucky. You're lucky. None of the working members voted for you—only the young people and young married couples. We'll try you for another month," and then he walked out. I was stunned. Later, many of the young married couples and the youth expressed their happiness that I would remain their pastor.

I continued to preach the Gospel and teach Bible doctrine. Outside of several adults in leadership positions in the church, the people encouraged us by their good response to the teaching of God's Word. Expressions of gratitude were received for our ministry, especially from the young married couples.

Several weeks later, the board chairman surprised me again by announcing that there would be a special board meeting that afternoon. As I looked over the congregation, I noticed that several board members who were very supportive of our ministry were out of town that Sunday. I immediately realized what was happening. The board chairman had seen his opportunity to get me, and he was going to take it. My hours were numbered.

There was a lot of small talk at the board meeting, as if they were working up the courage to ask for my resignation. Finally one man made the motion to ask me to resign effective that very night. One white haired man rose to his feet and said, "Brethren, I do not want to be a part of such action since this would be the third pastor fired by this board." After making his statement, he walked out of the room along with another board member. With these men resigning and other supporting board members absent that Sunday, I knew the jig was up. A motion for my dismissal was made and I was asked to announce my resignation that evening after the service. I hurried back to the parsonage to give Jackie the news and to begin preparing my resignation statement. In my heart I disliked being fired but at the same time I was beginning to see some light and a way out of this tunnel. The Lord knew that I put everything I had into this church ministry.

Jackie didn't say much, but supported me. I knew she would be happy to move again, even though she disliked moving. She was my encouragement, although in her heart, unknown to me, she always thought we would not be in West Virginia very long. She never told me her feelings until we left.

After that evening service, I announced that the board had asked for my resignation and that, effective immediately, I was no longer pastor of the church. It was like a bomb had been dropped. What an uproar! Church members cornered the board chairman and demanded an explanation. One lady suggested that the church was run like a Communist group. She said that they voted for me to come as pastor and that they supported my ministry financially so they should have a voice in whether I remain or be dismissed. Tensions and emotions put that congregation on the verge of a fight. The only way the chairman could calm the upset audience was to promise that the minutes of that board meeting would be read at the next Wednesday prayer service and the congregation could vote to accept or reject the board's decision.

That next Wednesday, the congregation heard the minutes of the board's decision and they voted down my dismissal. Now what were they going to do? In the frustration and confusion, the chairman was quick with a solution. He said that since I had already resigned, the church would take a vote in two weeks on whether to accept or reject my resignation. Then, for the next two weeks, Mr. M. busied himself with campaigning for people to come out for the vote and to vote against me. One lady who attended another church told me that the chairman had called her and asked her to come for the vote. She told him that if she came she would vote for me because she thought I was a nice guy. He then told her not to come.

The rumor mill was in high gear and the pressure was mounting. People would whisper when we walked by them at the country store, which also housed the post office. Some even parked their cars in front of the parsonage and watched our movements. There were times when Jackie and I tried to pray, but instead I cried because of the intense pressure. The mental stress and emotional pain became too great for Jackie since she was very pregnant with our third child, so we decided to go back to my parent's home in Blue Ball, Pennsylvania until the vote.

We returned to the parsonage on the day of the big vote. Since the parsonage was directly across the street from the church, I could watch the people gather. The chairman had certainly done a good job in getting people to come for the vote. I saw people pack into the church that I had never seen before. Our friends told me later that the chairman stood before the crowd and passed out ballots to all that came. He told them that they did not have to be a member of that church to vote, but they did have to be a Christian. If they were not a Christian, he said they could sign their name on the back of their ballot to become a Christian, and then they could vote.

To my amazement, after seeing so many strangers enter that church to vote, there was a majority of only three votes to accept my resignation. Some of those strangers had to have voted for me in order to make the results that close. And so, my ministry in West Virginia was finished, but God's plan was still intact.

After the vote, the parsonage was deluged with many friends who were upset and crying. One school teacher begged us to stay. She was willing to secure me a teaching job if I would stay and start a new church. I was not interested. I felt that my ministry, after six short months, was finished in that community. In fact, before leaving McConnell, I went over to the front door of the Tabernacle and literally shook the dust off of my feet. I was convinced that it was time for me to move on. I encouraged the remnant of the church to attend the local Baptist church up the street, which was pastored by a Moody Bible Institute graduate.

I learned many things the hard way through this experience. One thing I learned was that I was not called to be a pastor. I have great appreciation and admiration for pastors who faithfully preach the Word of God. I pray for pastors daily. My short experience as a pastor taught me much and I still carry the scars, but later I saw how God used my West Virginia church experience to prepare me for a greater ministry. It was a time of preparation. I prayed that I would be a quick learner during future times of preparation. F.B. Meyer said, "The main end of life is not to do but to become." My prayer was, "Make me, Lord, whatever you want me to be." Learning is a lifelong process.

A TIME OF WAITING

It was a very disturbing and emotional experience for me during our time in West Virginia. I was disillusioned about the pastorate and I really did not want to get involved with another church situation. Getting fired after only six months on the job did not help the résumé. I was wounded and worn out. Struggling with the forces of evil can be exhausting if one does not take on the whole armor of God. However, all of the wounds, struggles, and stress is lessened when we recognize that it is all part of God's plan in preparing us for that "prepared place" to minister. I have a better perspective now that I see West Virginia in the rear view mirror. I wouldn't want to go through that experience again for a million dollars, nor would I take a million dollars for that experience.

I knew God was working to prepare me for a "prepared place," but I didn't know where. With no job or ministry, our family of four returned home to my parents until we sorted things out. We needed time to heal and reflect. I took a job at the Trojan boat factory in Lancaster where every day I painted water lines and installed windshields on motor boats. It was boring, but I remembered someone saying that regardless of where God plants you, even if it is in a corner, let your light shine. I tried to be a witness for Christ in the factory. Some fellow employees questioned why I didn't have a better job since I had a college degree, while they never finished high school. At times it did seem like a waste of my training and time to be involved in such secular work. The Lord often brought to mind Dr. Bob Jones' chapel quote: "There is no difference between the secular and sacred because to the Christian all things are sacred and all ground is holy ground." Working in the boat factory was just another way God used to prepare my life for the future. Big things begin with little things.

While waiting for God's marching orders and unbeknown to me, someone suggested my name as a possible candidate for another church. I was frightened when I received that application for a church in Michigan. I didn't even want to complete the application but I felt compelled to because it might have been the Lord's next step for me. I was ready to march even if it was in a direction not of my choosing. Out of many applications the church received, I was one of three requested to candidate. I was horrified. Why would God put me into another church situation when I had failed in my first pastorate? I did not want anything to do with another church. I was hurt and the wounds were still very much in need of healing.

However, I consented to go and candidate because of the commitment that I had made years earlier to go wherever God wanted me to go. I was the second of the three candidates to preach in this Michigan church. I was told that they would call me with their decision after the third candidate preached. For two weeks I was in limbo. I was horrified every time the telephone rang, and would run out of the house. I did not want to answer it. I knew that if they chose me, I would have to go because it was God's marching orders. Finally the day of relief came when I received a letter informing me that another candidate had been chosen. It was quite an experience, but it was also a real test for me and the solidity of my commitment. Abraham made a commitment which involved offering his son Isaac as a sacrifice. Although Abraham did not want to sacrifice Isaac, he was prepared to do so. God intervened at the last minute with a sacrificial lamb relieving Abraham of the unthinkable. I felt God intervened in my situation by not sending me to another church.

While waiting for the Lord to open another door of service, my chiropractor friend Dr. Tom Berry suggested that I start a fifteen-minute daily devotional program on the local radio station. I felt a strong need to minister and tell people about the Lord Jesus Christ, which was what I had committed my life to do. When Dr. Berry said that he would pay for the radio time, I agreed and I started the radio broadcast over WGSA, Ephrata, PA. Every weekday morning, I would drive to Ephrata from Blue Ball to sign on at 7:00 a.m. over WGSA. It was a short devotional program that soon attracted many listeners. I was thrilled to receive mail which told of how God was using my broadcasts. When I started working at the boat factory, I had borrowed Dad's tape recorder and recorded the program in my bedroom. Working a full-time job in the boat factory and conducting a daily radio program was challenging, but God was preparing me for a larger radio ministry in the future. It was a great experience in discipline.

Throughout my early pilgrimage, little did I realize that sometimes there are the necessary painful processes of preparation for that prepared place. I knew that I had the responsibility to prepare for His service, so I studied His Word and prepared as best as I could. At the same time, God was preparing me for life. God uses prepared people. We do the applying but God does the work of preparation. God had several places of ministry prepared for me through which He prepared me for a larger ministry. Being faithful in little things makes us a candidate for bigger things. God is still at work in me preparing me for tomorrow, for eternity and beyond. I feel like I am just an ordinary guy in the hands of the extraordinary God.

The wisest man who ever lived said, *"How does a man become wise? The first step is to trust and reverence the Lord! Only fools refuse to be taught. Listen to your father and mother. What you learn from them will stand you in good stead; it will gain you many honors"* (Proverbs 1:7-9 LB).

PHOTOS

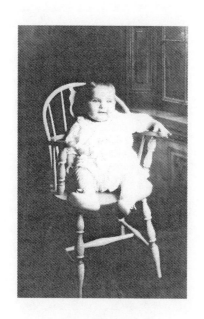

1 – BABY DICK

HAPPY SCHOOL DAYS
1937

2 – FIRST GRADE

3 – DICK & BROTHER GLENN

4 – BOB JONES UNIVERSITY FRESHMAN

5 – DICK'S 1949 PONTIAC

6 – DICK'S PARENTS – ABE & ANNA

7 – DICK & JACKIE'S WEDDING

8 – SNAVELY FAMILY (1968)
Randy, Carol Ann, Rick
Ron, Jackie, Dick

9 – FIRST YFC OFFICE (NAPLES, NY)

10 – YFC OFFICE (AVOCA, NY)

11 – YFC CENTER GROUNDBREAKING (1966)

12 – JONI ERICKSON TADA RALLY

13 – YFC CENTER (KANONA, NY)

14 – YFC CENTER (KANONA, NY)

15 – PERFORMING ARTS PRODUCTION

16 – FIRST SHARATHON (1984)

17 – THE BROADCASTER

18 – YOUTH CAMP (LETOURNEAU)

PART II

MINISTRY

8

☙ ❧

GOD'S PLAN BEGINS TO UNFOLD

AN OPPORTUNITY

IT WAS THE EARLY PART of 1957 when Dick Coons, my old friend from BJU, entered my life again. The Billy Graham Evangelistic Film Association had sent Dad to Rochester, NY to operate the large Kodak arc projector used to show one of the Graham films for a large Youth for Christ rally. At this rally, Dad crossed paths with Dick, who was now the executive director of Rochester Youth for Christ. He evidently remembered me because when he learned that this Billy Graham Film Representative was my Dad, he asked Dad what I was doing. Dad told him that I was working in a boat factory while waiting on the Lord for opportunities to minister. Dick mentioned that some men in the Southern Tier of New York were considering a Youth for Christ program, and he wondered if I might be interested in such an opportunity.

When Dad returned home and told me about the possibilities of starting a youth ministry, my ears perked up. At that time, I had the daily radio program and did some preaching in area churches while working in the boat factory. In my heart I knew that there had to be something else. Here was an opportunity to establish a not-for-profit organization and work with youth.

I was excited and eager to learn more. I began to dream of what I could do to get a youth ministry started. I remembered that Dr. Gilbert Stenholm, BJU Dean of the School of Religion, had suggested that I might consider becoming a minister with Youth for Christ after graduation, and now I couldn't wait to make contact with Dick Coons. I was excited about the great possibilities of serving the Lord in this capacity. I was like a soldier ready to jump at my Commander's call; though I have to admit, I was hoping that it was not a call to pastor a church. The scars of my West Virginia church experience were still very fresh.

I immediately wrote to Dick Coons, informing him of my interest. He suggested that I meet with him to discuss this opportunity and, within a week or two, I found myself in Rochester, NY. We renewed our friendship and talked at length about how a YFC organization functioned. I spent the night with Dick and his family, and we talked more the following morning. Dick told me that he had conducted some youth rallies in the rural Southern Tier and that there was a lot of interest and enthusiasm among adults and youth. He said that many teenagers from this area attended his Rochester YFC summer camp programs at the LeTourneau Christian Camp on Canandaigua Lake every summer. He answered many of my questions about Rochester Youth for Christ operations and how he raised money to finance the organization. He assured me that he would help me if I were willing to take a leap of faith and organize a youth ministry. I told him one of my concerns was how to raise the money necessary to start and maintain such a youth ministry. I was not interested if I had to beg people for money for this new venture. My philosophy for financing God's programs has always been, "What God orders, He pays for." I tell God about the need, tell His people about the need, ask God to speak to His people about giving, and then pray that His people will be obedient and give as God directs them.

Dick assured me that I wouldn't have to beg people for money, and having this assurance from him, I said that I would be willing to step out on faith and trust the Lord to give me—just an ordinary guy—extraordinary wisdom and strength. I knew I needed these to develop an organization to reach people, especially teenagers, with the Gospel. This certainly sounded more exciting than painting water lines and installing windshields on motor boats.

Dick made plans the following day to drive 45 miles south to Naples, where he introduced me to Mr. Selby Smith. Selby and his wife owned a nursing home in Naples. Selby was the real motivator behind this idea of organizing a YFC ministry. He was a very big man with a very big heart, and he would do anything to help young people. For that matter, he would truly give the shirt off of his back to help anyone in need. He had been coordinating hymn sings in the area churches. In 1956, in this rural area of western New York, there were very few places for Christian teens to go for fun and fellowship, and, as there was not much to do on Sunday evenings following church services, hymn sings became very popular. These hymn sings would rotate from church to church, and young people would gather to sing hymns and gospel choruses and fellowship with teenagers from other churches. This arrangement created a much larger crowd than any of the small rural churches could muster on their own, and this larger circle of Christian youth made it more exciting. Many new friends were made as teenagers met other teens outside of their own denomination.

During this time, I dreamed about the ministry every night, and my thoughts were continually on it every day. After meeting with Selby Smith and getting to know him and his passion to reach teenagers with the Gospel, Selby decided to make arrangements for me to meet a group of the men and area pastors who were active in the hymn sings. Selby said that these men were deeply concerned about the spiritual needs of youth in the area, and they could be very helpful. On May 27, 1957, I met with these men at the Pleasant Valley Manor restaurant near Hammondsport, NY to explore the idea of beginning some sort of youth ministry. It was wonderful to meet pastors and laymen from different denominations who shared a common interest in ministering to youth. The group consisted of businessmen, school teachers, pastors, farmers, a dentist, a carpenter, and other laymen. We all sat around a very long table and fellowshipped over a delicious meal. Each one expressed his desire to work together for the sake of area youth. They asked me many questions regarding my family, education, organizational skills, and ministry experiences.

After a time of fellowship and sharing, it was decided to set up a youth rally where I would preach an evangelistic message to the youth. The group was interested to see if I could communicate with teenagers. Selby Smith was the mover and shaker in this group of men and after the meeting he told me that he was confident that I would be the one to organize and direct an effective youth ministry. He informed me early in our relationship that he was one who rushes in where angels fear to tread. I found that to be very true, but his heart was right. He was a praying man. He was an encourager and a blessing to many, and he would often meet with me to pray about needs and ask God's blessings upon this ministry.

After the meeting in Hammondsport, I drove home excited about the possibilities of helping these men organize a YFC ministry. The excitement and anticipation kept me awake for the six-hour drive. My mind wandered, and a vision of this ministry began developing in my mind. All kinds of ideas came to me on that trip back home. I prayed for God's wisdom and direction as I drove those many miles. I was confident, with God's help, that we could do the job. I didn't have all of the answers, but I started to believe that this was the place for which God had been preparing me. I couldn't wait to tell Jackie as I knew she was praying for me. The following day, I shared the highlights of my trip with her. She was excited too, and her positive attitude over the next few days became more of a confirmation to me.

A few days later Selby called and informed me that he had scheduled the youth rally where I was to be introduced to the youth in the area. The rally was set for June 29, 1957 at the Arkport Central School. Mr. Howard Benning, one of the men who worked behind the scenes to help this fledging young man get this ministry off the ground, made the arrangements to use the school gym.

The day of my introduction arrived. Selby Smith set up the order of the program and was the emcee. He informed me in no uncertain terms, that we had to be finished by 9:00 p.m. These were the arrangements agreed upon with the school janitor, and it was stressed to me that this was critical because running over could jeopardize our future use of this school. This experience is one I shall never forget.

I felt intense pressure as I sat on the stage looking out onto an audience of about two hundred people, mostly teenagers. I felt as if everyone was watching my every move. The gym was steaming hot, and the crowd was restless because of the heat. Because the program lacked continuity and organization, it was dragging and time was wasting away. I wanted so badly to get up, lead a chorus, and put some life and enthusiasm into the program, but it was not my turn. Instead, I watched that clock hanging on the gym wall like I had never watched a clock before. The minutes were rapidly ticking away while some teenagers provided special music. Then someone led the audience in a few choruses. The clock was still ticking toward that nine o'clock deadline. Then it was time for announcements, which were boring. Next came the offering, and that clock never slowed down. I wanted to make a good impression on the audience. I wanted to do my best for God's glory. I wanted the Lord to be honored. I wanted teenagers to hear the Gospel, but I was afraid I wouldn't have time to do anything other than say "hello."

I looked at what remained on the program agenda, and I calculated that we were not going to make that deadline unless I cut my message short—really short. There were 20 minutes remaining, then ten, and finally we came to the last special music. Afterward, Selby Smith stood up to introduce me, and as I walked to the podium, he whispered to me, "Take what time you need." As I stood before that audience and looked at that clock, I saw that I had less than five minutes to present myself and to deliver a Gospel message to teenagers. It was a short message that had already been mentally condensed several times. I prayed for wisdom and strength.

I don't remember many things about that rally because of the great concern and pressure that I had about meeting that time deadline. Because our program ran over, it was the last time we were able to use that school, and I felt badly for Howard Benning because he had made the arrangements with the school officials and the janitor.

I discovered later that I did not make the best of impressions on at least one of the committee members. Harry Rung is a fun guy, and since those early days, we have had many laughs about his first impression of me at that rally. He told me many years later what he had told the committee that very evening: "This guy will never make it as a youth leader. With his bald head, he looks like an old man." I was twenty-six years old, and being bald at a very early age was considered a disadvantage for a youth worker. However, the committee faced a dilemma in that I was their only candidate for the challenging job of establishing and managing an organization to minister to youth. Regardless of how old-looking this young whippersnapper appeared and how inexperienced I was, God had a plan, and I was part of that plan. God uses us not according to our outward appearance but, rather, according to our heart, commitment, and obedience. To God be all of the glory.

A CHALLENGE ACCEPTED

A few days later, I received a call from Selby Smith informing me that the committee was asking me if I would, indeed, come and develop a ministry and organization to reach youth for Jesus Christ. This was an opportunity to meet a need with the organizational and ministry tools with which God had blessed me.

It did not take long for me to give an answer because Jackie and I had been praying about this challenge. I was anxious and ready to charge full speed ahead. As an entrepreneur at heart, it seemed to be a real fit. I loved to organize and plan. I enjoyed sharing my faith with anyone who would listen. So, I began to dream how to raise funds, how to organize a board of directors, how to begin Bible clubs, etc. I was charting new territory, but I knew the Lord would guide and direct me so long as I kept my eyes and heart on Him and so long as I remembered to give Him all of the glory.

My first challenge was to move all of our furniture to New York in the cheapest way possible, as we had very little money. My good friend, chiropractor Dr. Tom Berry, was so kind to let us use his barn, and our furniture was stored there for many months. The sofa made an excellent nest for the rats and mice, we later discovered. His son Dan Berry, a dear brother in the Lord, helped me drive the rental truck from Strasburg, PA to Naples, NY. When the truck was loaded, we committed the trip to the Lord in prayer and started down the highway. By the time we got to Williamsport, PA, it was pitch dark. We were munching on some snack food when, halfway up the mountain north of Williamsport, the truck engine began to sputter and finally quit. We were out of gas. The truck rental company assured me that there would be enough gas to get us to our destination. We had prayed for protection on this trip and now here we were, dangerously sitting on the side of a mountain. There was no room to pull off to the side of the road, so we were stopped in the middle of a two lane road on busy US Route 15. It was scary.

How and where could we get gasoline at this late hour while sitting in the dark on this mountain side? Southbound cars and trucks barely saw us, and they narrowly missed us as they sped by. Dan had a little flashlight to warn cars that were coming up the mountain behind us. While praying and asking the Lord for help and wisdom, He suddenly reminded me that there were two gas tanks on this truck, and I began trying to figure out how to turn on the second tank of gasoline. We turned the headlights on only when we heard a car or truck coming down the mountain. Otherwise, the lights were off to conserve the battery. We were determined that the enemy was not going to win this frightening battle of frustration and discouragement. This was really a time for watching and praying. At last we found how to open the second tank. We finally pumped the throttle to where we got enough gas to the carburetor, and the engine fired up. We praised the Lord, and slowly crept up the mountain with our heavy load. If this was supposed to be a discouraging episode, it didn't work. I was committed to this new call upon my life, and now with a full tank of gas we were on our way rejoicing and thanking the Lord for His protection. Obstacles thrown in our pathway are tests and trials that we must conquer to gain the beautiful victory that lies ahead.

At last, we made it to the house we were going to rent in Naples, NY and after unloading the furniture, we returned the truck to Lancaster, PA without incident. Our house was divided into two apartments, side by side. We lived in one, and a young couple lived on the other. It was a small white house owned by a German couple from Rochester. The house had a floor furnace in one room that provided heat for the entire apartment. The kitchen had white metal cabinets and very little storage area. The bathroom was off the kitchen, while all of the bedrooms were on the second floor. Linoleum covered the floors in all of the rooms on both first and second floors. The clothes washer and dryer were located in an attached building that had no heat, causing them to freeze up in the cold winters. The housing conditions were not much to write home about, but it was a place to live, and we were thankful for that.

We settled into this house on Weld Street, which mostly consisted of old wooden framed houses. Our neighbors were very cordial, and, of course, we wanted to befriend them and show forth a good Christian testimony. One neighbor across the street had a little boy about a year older than our son, Rickie, and he always seemed to be getting into some kind of trouble. One day, the two boys wandered right into the meticulously kept garden in our neighbor's yard, and for reasons unknown to this day, they proceeded to pull out all of the carrots. When we were politely informed of this incident by the neighbor, we were dumbfounded and embarrassed. We made certain that Rickie knew what he did was wrong, and after administering some disciplinary action, Rickie went to the neighbor and apologized. So much for getting off to a positive start with our neighbors.

It was August 1957 when, at the age of 26, Jackie and I, along with three children, Carol Ann, Rickie, and Randy, settled in Naples. Later, our son Ron was born, completing our family. Only six years had passed since making the acquaintance of Dick Coons in South Carolina, and here I was in New York State beginning the ministry of Area Youth for Christ, which is now called Family Life Ministries. God had a plan even in the little things, like making an acquaintance at a dinner table. Every appointment is a divine appointment for the Christian.

YFC BEGINS

After a couple of days of unpacking boxes and setting up what little crude furniture we had, I was off to my first ministry event. While Jackie was getting things settled in the house, I went to the LeTourneau Christian Camp on Canandaigua Lake, where Rochester YFC was beginning ten days of summer camp. A few teens from the Naples area were campers at the Rochester YFC camp, so I had a vested interest in being there.

Originally, my primary function for the week was to observe how Dick Coons and his staff conducted the camp program. I was ready and eager to learn all that I could. However, a few hours after I arrived at camp, I was informed that the sports director had canceled out, and I found myself appointed sports director for the week. I was really shocked. I knew nothing about being a sports director, plus I couldn't find my way around the campground yet. There is nothing like learning on the job, especially when you are thrown into it at the last minute. Once again, I called upon the Lord to help me. I asked a few questions about what was expected of the sports director, and then I immediately jumped in with both feet and got involved. The camp was divided into teams which played ping pong, basketball, softball, volleyball, held swimming contests, and participated in other activities. Points were earned for wins, as well as for memorizing Bible verses. Our goal was to create a lot of competition and enthusiasm with the sports program, and the teenagers were very responsive. They were screaming and yelling at the end of each day when their teams' scores were announced during the evening rallies. We had a great but exhausting time at camp, and at the end, Dick Coons thanked me for a job well done. It was gratifying to know that I had won the respect and friendship of many teenagers. That would not have happened if I were only an observer as originally planned. God's plan is always better than man's plan.

Camp concluded on Labor Day weekend, and the following week I began organizing Hi-C (High School Christian) Bible Clubs at schools all across the area. I went to schools to meet with Christian students who formed the nucleus of our club program. I went wherever I could find some Christian teens to promote the clubs and activities. One time, I met with Connie Ladue, a farm girl, out in the field on her tractor to plan a club meeting in her high school. We were starting from scratch, so I had a lot of "selling" to do.

A NEAR DISASTER

If the first YFC rally was to be any indication of the future success of this organization, most would have predicted it was going to be a disaster. Arrangements for this rally were made in advance of my arrival to New York. The committee member who made the arrangements misunderstood and, because of this, miscommunicated some vital information. Announcements were made about using the Arkport school auditorium, but no one ever cleared the date with the school officials. All of a sudden, some last minute negotiations had to be made, and thanks again to Howard Benning, we were able to use the Arkport Methodist Church on short notice. It was the first and only of our rallies ever to be held in a church building, but it was our salvation for that rally.

That evening I started the rally program with some lively singing. I always enjoyed leading congregational singing and in those early days we had two exceptional ladies who played the piano with gusto—Jean Buckley from Naples and Lois Dungan of Arkport. Both were regulars at the piano for YFC. For many years, Lois played at all of the YFC functions wherever they were held. The special teen music for this first rally was well received. We made the announcements and took up an offering while waiting for the speaker, a Christian college president, to arrive. When Robin Adair, one of the committee members who had made the arrangements with the speaker, called to check on him, he discovered that he was sitting at home watching TV. He had completely forgotten about this engagement! Committee members scurried around wondering what to do, while I led an extra long song service to allow time for the speaker to arrive. Finally a note was given to me in the middle of a song informing me that the speaker was not coming. It was followed by another note suggesting we use a missionary candidate in the audience who would be glad to speak. I had to make a fast decision while leading the rally in song, so I decided to go with the missionary. I quickly introduced him, and he then he spoke for about twenty-five minutes concerning his mission field. He meant well, but I knew he wasn't really connecting with the teenagers. I feared our first rally would be a disaster unless somehow we regained their attention. While the missionary was still speaking, I began thinking how I could bridge his thoughts with a salvation message to this crowd of young people. When the missionary was finished, I gave a very brief Gospel message. God blessed, and in spite of our blunders, there were several teenagers who committed their lives to Christ that evening. God had a plan, and even though it appeared that the enemy tried to upset those plans, God was glorified.

I began planning youth activities and youth rallies for every Saturday night in different high school auditoriums, grange halls, town halls and any building we could find. I quickly learned that two effective methods of reaching teenagers are sports and music. Many of our Saturday night youth rallies included music groups from area colleges as well as local teenagers. One of the sports programs that was a big hit with everyone was a Judo team from Bob Jones University. We scheduled the team in several high schools during the week, where they presented some Judo demonstrations and then promoted the big Judo program at the YFC rally on Saturday night. Hundreds of teenagers attended this rally, with many responding to the Gospel message the team gave.

MEAGER BEGINNINGS

From that first committee of interested men, a board of directors evolved, and in November 1957, we were incorporated as a

501(c)(3) not-for-profit corporation in New York State. Our first annual budget was $7,140 and included everything from postage, film rentals, speaker honorariums, printing, rent, supplies, etc. My salary of $55 per week was also included, provided sufficient funds were received through offerings and contributions. This was half of my former salary, but by faith Jackie and I accepted the challenge, convinced that the Lord would provide in some way. Jackie was always ready and willing to go with me wherever I believed God was leading me. She never complained, even when we faced some difficult times financially. She encouraged and helped me. Whenever there was a need for secretarial work at the office, she was ready and willing to help. She typed letters, stuffed envelopes, answered the phone, and did interior decorating in the offices. She has always been my best critic in a positive way because of her intense desire to see me succeed in whatever God called me to do, and she has always tried her best to make me look good in every way. She has been one of the reasons for the success of this ministry. The Lord used her to help me, just an ordinary guy, to prepare for God's work. She was part of God's plan.

Selby Smith owned an abandoned property in Naples where he allowed me to set up the first YFC office, and it looked like a haunted house. Situated on a lofty site at the corner of Elizabeth and Vine Streets, it was weatherworn and very much in need of paint. It had been unoccupied for several years and was completely gutted down to the wall studs. There were no bathroom facilities or plumbing. It was originally planned to be the living quarters for our family, but it was obviously not in livable condition. Therefore, we used the front room of this house for our YFC office. There was no rent, but neither was there any heat. Selby gave me a glass electric space heater which I placed in front of my little kneehole desk during that first winter. It kept the chill off and we survived. My office equipment included that electric heater, a small kneehole desk, a telephone, a filing cabinet, and a portable typewriter that I used in college.

Nearly every morning, Selby would come by the office to pray with me for the ministry. He was a real prayer warrior. One day I was shocked when I arrived at the office and found him on the floor, stretched out flat on his back with his huge belly protruding upward like a mountain. What a sight! I thought he had had a heart attack and wondered how I would ever move him in that condition. Suddenly, he awoke, saw me looking down on him, and smiled. He was just taking a nap before I arrived to meet with him for prayer. We prayed for miracles—lots of them. Selby always prayed for big things. He talked big, he thought big, and he warned me that he had big ideas. Selby not only prayed for big things, but he also gave big, especially that first year when we were just getting off the ground. His four children were involved with YFC, but his wife was not always supportive of his involvement with us and, at times, I felt like his counselor as he shared some deep personal problems. In spite of our good relationship, his YFC involvement slowly faded in order to keep peace at home.

Selby's old house was also the site of our first radio broadcasts. I contacted some local radio stations for some free air time for a YFC radio program. Two radio stations, WHHO, Hornell and WCKR, Dundee, agreed to air a half-hour YFC radio broadcast every Saturday afternoon, and we produced and recorded the radio program in that old abandoned and gutted house that we used as my office. We hung blankets around the room to prevent any echoes as we made a joyful noise. The Davis quartet of Middlesex, NY, gathered around a mike and provided the special music. Mrs. Pat Elwell accompanied the quartet on the same Hammond spinet organ that Selby transported from school to school on Saturday nights. Following the music selections, I made announcements of YFC rallies and then gave a brief devotional. After the tape recordings were made, I personally delivered the tapes to the radio stations for the Saturday Youth for Christ broadcasts.

I began spending very little time in that office as I was on the road organizing Hi-C Clubs, scheduling high school auditoriums for Saturday night rallies, contacting pastors, receipting donations, and a host of other things. Hi-C Clubs were organized in fifteen area high schools in Ontario, Livingston, Yates and Steuben Counties. Throughout the years, we had clubs in Hornell, Naples, Middlesex, Cohocton, Wayland, Prattsburgh, Dansville, Avoca, Bath, Canisteo, Jasper, Greenwood, Troupsburg, Addison, Corning, Buena Vista, Arkport, Canaseraga, Almond, Dundee, Bradford, Savona, Campbell, and Nunda. The Clubs met weekly during lunch hour, after school, or in the evening. I was literally running from morning until night on weekdays and then producing and directing a youth rally every Saturday night in a different location. Besides producing the radio programs every Saturday, I also prepared the copy material for our monthly publication of the YFC NEWS for the printers. At the same time, I preached for many pastors who needed someone to fill their pulpits on Sundays.

Many wonderful people often fed me supper as I ran from one club meeting to the next. After my afternoon club in Jasper, Dick and Winnie Price always invited me to stay for supper with their family. This saved me a trip home, since my next club meeting was in Buena Vista that evening. On Monday evenings, I would often have supper with Bruce and Lois Dungan following the Arkport club meeting. Bruce was chairman of the YFC board, and we often did some business following a few rousing games of ping pong in the basement.

That first year in Naples proved to be exciting and challenging in many ways. A spiritual coldness was prevalent, and we were not very well-received. Some Naples churches felt threatened, fearing that YFC would take young people and money away from their congregations. A rumor spread in the community that YFC was a communist organization and that YFC really stood for Youth for Communism. We were looked upon with suspicion as a new organization in town. It was frustrating and discouraging at times, but we did not dwell on the negatives. We kept our minds focused on the mission of reaching teenagers with the Gospel.

About a week or two into my new responsibilities, I received a telephone call from Board Member Robin Adair one morning at 6:00 a.m., questioning me as to why I was not at the office working. He informed me that I was not being paid to sleep in every morning. Not knowing Robin Adair very well, I was a little concerned that maybe I was really expected to be in the office at that early hour. I soon found out that Mr. Adair enjoyed such pranks, and I quickly learned how to cope with his humor. Our small kids really liked him because once in a while he would take us all out to a restaurant for a Sunday dinner—a real treat at a time when eating out was a luxury in our family.

We did find fellowship that first year in a small Pentecostal group of about a dozen people who met in an old church building. It was owned by one man, and the owner made all of the decisions regarding the use of the building. A young couple, Noah Stoltzfus and his wife Edie, were recent graduates of Elim Bible Institute in Lima, NY, and they were pastoring this small flock of believers. They were committed to Christ, and we found great fellowship with them. They were so encouraging to us spiritually and socially, and we shared many things in common since we both came from Lancaster County. Together, we had great fun, fellowship and laughs.

One day, before Pastor Noah was ordained, he asked me to perform a marriage ceremony for a couple in the church. This was only the second marriage ceremony I had ever performed, so it was a memorable occasion. I had just met the couple before the service. The groom was trembling, and the bride's hands were shaking as we discussed the ceremony. I was nervous, but I remembered I was doing this for my Brother Noah's sake. I read the ceremony from a pastoral handbook—the same script I had used in the previous ceremony, including the names of the previous bride and groom. How embarrassing to discover that I had failed to insert the names of this new couple. Fortunately, they stopped me before it was too late.

The first year for our family in New York and for this new YFC organization was difficult, but God was with us. That was all that I needed to know. Money was not always available to meet my salary. Two or three times we existed a whole month without a paycheck, and there were real financial struggles, but God always provided in other ways. Many times, His provisions were unique.

Once, I received a check for an odd amount from my father. He explained that a policeman had stopped him for speeding, and he promised the Lord to send me the fine money if he didn't have to pay the fine. On another occasion, we had some missionary friends unexpectedly stop by for a visit and I invited them to stay for lunch. My wife was in the kitchen and, after hearing my invitation she gave me a look that told me that something was drastically wrong. I was always very sensitive to those looks, as Jackie can use them to communicate volumes. I excused myself and headed to the kitchen where my wife informed me that we didn't have anything to feed our guests. No food and no money made it very difficult to break bread with a missionary friend. I realized that I had a problem, but I quickly gave it to the Lord.

Board Member Selby Smith came to my mind, and I made a trip down the street to his house and asked to borrow a quart of milk and a can of soup. I didn't tell him what I wanted it for but said that I would return it. That afternoon, we all had tomato soup for lunch. Although the soup was rather watery, our guests never knew anything was wrong. God had a plan for my plight.

Another time, I invited some friends to our house for refreshments and fellowship after the Saturday night rally. On the way home I told Jackie about these friends coming to our house and she informed me that we did not have refreshments to serve. Here was another jam I found myself in because I had failed to consult with my wife. When our friends arrived, we sat around the table. I informed them that all we had to serve them were the mixed nuts that were in a bowl in the middle of the table, and then I prayed and thanked the Lord for the nuts. We began shelling nuts and fellowshipping, and this became one of those memorable moments that our friends have talked about for years.

In spite of the difficult financial times that first year, I never once questioned God. I was too busy doing what I believed in my heart God had called me to do. Every Monday morning I would take the Saturday night rally offering to our treasurer, Mr. Gerald Margeson. He would pay all of the bills and if any money was left over, it went toward my salary. After that first year, we never missed a paycheck, nor have any of our staff members ever missed a paycheck because of a lack of funds. "What God orders, He pays for." I am convinced that if we do God's work in God's way and for God's glory, it will have God's provisions and blessings. The Scriptures say, *"The Lord's blessing is our greatest wealth"* (Proverbs 10:22 LB).

MY FIRST NEW YORK SNOW STORM

Another challenge that year was our first winter in New York State. I have always loved snow, and I was told that this area has some big snowstorms. I told people that I was praying for ten feet of snow that year. Well, I got what I prayed for. One snowy morning I went to the office, checked the mail, and answered some correspondence before hitting the road to meet with the Hi-C Club kids. On this particular day, I had a club in Jasper after school and then Buena Vista/Canisteo in the evening. It continued to snow all afternoon. I was able to meet with the Jasper Club, after which I always had supper with Mr. Richard Price, his wife Winnie, and their children. Dick was a schoolteacher in Jasper, a YFC board member, and later YFC board chairman. He really did a lot for me and the YFC organization in those early days. His sweet wife, Winnie, was always so accommodating.

After eating supper with the Price family, I headed to Buena Vista in my 1955 Eighty-Eight Oldsmobile.

Being new to the area, I was not familiar with all of the back roads. The snow was very heavy and the winds were creating large drifts. I made it to Canisteo, but the snow was blowing and drifting as I turned up Stephen's Gulch. It was getting difficult to see, but I knew I had to keep going, thinking kids would be waiting for me. Suddenly, I realized that I had made a wrong turn; I should have turned onto Baker's Gulch. I couldn't stop. I couldn't turn around. I had to keep up my momentum because the snow was getting very deep.

I assumed that once I got to the north end of Stephen's Gulch, I could take a connecting road to Baker's Gulch, and that would bring me down to Buena Vista. Unbeknownst to me, I was now traveling on a seasonal road that was literally abandoned in the winter season. Suddenly, I hit a large snowdrift right in the middle of the road. Snow flew everywhere. I was stuck, and I knew that I was stuck for good when I got my flashlight out and saw the snow was so packed underneath my car that it had raised the chassis. Getting out of there was going to be a long ordeal. I began to wonder what God's plan was now.

It was dark. It was cold. It was snowing and blowing, and I was all alone and lost. I saw a small shed by the road and thought I might find shelter in it. After examining it with my flashlight, I discovered it was an empty pigpen. The snow was heavy and getting very deep. No lights could be seen anywhere. I considered walking, but I was not sure of the terrain or where I really was located. With half of a tank of gasoline, I decided it would be safer to spend the night in the car and run the engine sparingly to conserve on the gasoline. I checked to be sure that the snow was cleaned away from the exhaust pipe to prevent asphyxiation as I remembered recent reports of people dying in their cars in snowstorms. I didn't want to become a statistic.

I was too anxious to sleep that night as I prayed for a snowplow to come. I did not realize that I was on a road where the plows never do come in the winter.

When I started to chill, I would start the engine to get some heat. I was only wearing a short jacket. Fortunately, I had a candy bar that I slowly consumed during the long night. I drifted in and out of sleep. When daylight came, the snow had drifted around my car and had covered the hood and part of the windshield. I turned the radio on to WHAM, the Rochester radio station, to get a weather report. I was taken aback when they reported that there would be snow, high winds, and drifting snow all day long.

I decided that I had to find help and get to safety before I got completely buried in snow. I had a small pair of boots and my light jacket. Since I did not have a hat for my bald head, I took the terrycloth seat cover off the front seat of the car, wrapped it around my head and neck, and started walking. It was more like climbing through the snow. I approached several houses only to find them abandoned. I discovered that walking in snow over four feet deep is quite a bit of exercise.

After knocking on the doors of several abandoned homes, I decided to head north, believing that sooner or later, I would come to the town of Howard. I walked a few steps and then stopped to catch my breath, with the snow beating against my face from the high winds. It was a blizzard like I had never witnessed. To keep on what I thought was the road, I tried to follow a row of fence posts that were barely sticking out of the snow. The blowing snow cut my visibility, but I continued slowly on what I hoped was the road. Suddenly, I saw the faint outline of a house. I did not get my hopes up because of my disappointment in finding the other houses vacant. While clawing my way toward this farmhouse, I saw a shed, and there were noises coming from it. I listened harder. Those sounds were from a pen full of pigs. What a beautiful sound! I was excited because I had found something living in that blizzard and thought that perhaps this farmhouse would not be abandoned. I knocked on the front door but received no answer. Then I saw an enclosed stairway at the side of the house and climbed the steps, hoping to find someone. I must have been quite a sight to the couple who opened the door and invited me in. My eyebrows were thick with snow and ice, my face fire engine red, and I was totally exhausted.

This dear couple made me some hot chocolate and a good breakfast, and listened to my story. I called my wife and told her what had happened. Jackie had been up all night, and now she cried with relief. Selby Smith had called the police and road crews, asking them to search for me. Dick Price had traveled the road from Jasper, where I had my last Bible club meeting, towards my next intended stop in Buena Vista. He looked down over banks and anywhere else that I might have fallen into. Pastor Wally Taylor of the Buena Vista Wesleyan Church was also out searching for me since I had failed to show up for the Buena Vista Bible Club meeting. Of course, neither Dick Price nor Pastor Taylor could ever have found me since I was off my intended route. The local radio stations were announcing that I was lost and were asking for help in locating me.

This farm where I finally found refuge was at the end of the road for winter travel and snow plowing. That morning, after the snowplow cleared a route to this farm house, YFC Board Chairman Selby Smith came to pick me up and take me home. As I walked in the door of our house, I was greeted by my loving wife and kids. I thanked the Lord for saving me and spent the rest of the day at home watching it snow and catching up on some sleep. Four days later, large snow blowers found my car, which was nearly covered by drifting snow. I can honestly say that I never really feared during this whole ordeal because I was convinced that God was with me. He had a plan, and this was part of my training.

9

❧ ❧

YFC GROWS

AFTER ONE YEAR OF being located in the abandoned house, the YFC office was moved to Main Street in Naples on the second floor of the Naples Pharmacy. My workload increased, and Mrs. Bertha Dillon of Ingleside graciously volunteered her services as office secretary. She was such a generous lady and was very interested in our work, especially since her daughter was a teenager and involved in the youth ministry. Bertha typed my letters, receipted contributions, answered the phone, and took care of most of the office details.

In 1960, the Woodworth family, consisting of Miss Ruth Woodworth, who was a veteran missionary, and her sisters, offered to sell their house in Avoca, NY to YFC. With the recent death of their parents, they were anxious to keep the house in Christian hands, and they made an appealing offer to the YFC board. It was suggested that the large house could provide space for the YFC office, as well as living quarters for the director's family. It was a huge undertaking for this small two-year-old ministry. We had no debts, but we also had no money in the bank, so buying real estate was not on the agenda. We were just able to keep our heads above water financially, but, as the

Woodworth offer was so attractive, the YFC board discussed the matter at the next monthly board meeting. After much discussion, a motion was made to purchase the property. However, there was one problem. Two board members were not in agreement with the move. When the board chairman asked me for my opinion, I told the board that I was very happy either way, but that I was concerned that there was not total unity on the board in making such a big decision.

The board, being very sensitive to the lack of unanimity, decided to vote again, and the decision was unanimous to reject the Woodworth offer. I was impressed and very grateful for the spirit and attitude of the men comprising this board of directors. After several weeks, I had the opportunity to sit down with the two opposing board members, and we discussed the pros and cons of the house offer. Their concern was that the headquarters of the organization would be moved out of Naples. My concern was a debt load, but when we all realized that our financial costs of renting or ownership were about the same, we began to see the wisdom of accepting the Woodworth's very favorable offer. Together, we earnestly prayed for God's will to be done at the next board meeting.

When the Woodworth house did not sell, the family came back with an even better offer. The two opposing board members spoke up and said that they were now in favor of the purchase. The YFC board voted again, and this time it was a unanimous vote to purchase the house. I have always appreciated the board's desire for unity. Over the years, when there were times of big decisions and there was not total unanimity, the board chairman would call for further discussion or table the matter. *"Where the Spirit of the Lord is, there is liberty (unity)"* (II Corinthians 3:17 KJV).

The beautiful stone and brick house on the corners of Alexander, Maple, and Lyon Streets in Avoca was purchased for $7,500 with a $500 down payment. The Woodworth family carried the mortgage at 4% interest, with YFC agreeing to pay a minimum of $500 annually on the principal.

The newly acquired house was well-built and solid, but it needed some major modernization and improvements. The 30" x 18" steel kitchen sink was located in a corner next to the outside door of the kitchen. The kitchen was illuminated with a single 75 watt light bulb swinging on an electrical cord hanging from the ceiling. The bathroom, with its steel bathtub, was located next to the kitchen. The kitchen cupboards were four feet deep and ran from the floor to the ceiling. When some of the ladies saw the antiquated kitchen, they felt sorry for Jackie. A close friend, Janet Benning, said, "Poor Jackie! She is going to live like a pioneer woman."

There were three additional rooms downstairs, all with very high ceilings. The beautiful wooden staircase inside the front door led to four bedrooms and a storage room upstairs. Board Member Gerald Margeson and his helper, Mr. Vernon Parker, went to work remodeling the house. With the removal of a couple of partitions downstairs, the front room became the new YFC office. With Jackie's interior decorating skills, the balance of the house became a very nice residence for our family.

Every month, the board of directors would meet in our living room for prayer and business. At times, the meetings were quite lengthy, but there was always time for everyone to pray. At one meeting, while everyone was on his knees, the brother who prayed first fell asleep by the time we had prayed around the circle. He began to snore, and after the last man prayed, as the men began to get up off of their knees, this brother woke up and began praying again. It was humorous but embarrassing for the sleepy brother. I guess he was praying "in snoozing and out of snoozing."

In so many ways, Jackie has always stood by my side, praying, helping, and encouraging me. She always prepared refreshments for each board meeting. It was usually a special dessert, and the board always looked forward to her refreshments, which ranged from strawberry shortcake to ice cream sundaes to pie-a-la-mode. Board Member Alan Archer always said that every time I had a project for board approval, Jackie would bring on the refreshments. Alan called it "The Snavely Snow Job," and it became a standing joke for many years.

GREATER ELMIRA YFC

God was blessing our efforts with youth and was opening other doors where we could share what He was teaching us. In 1961, a few pastors in the Greater Elmira area asked if we could help them organize a YFC ministry in their area. It reminded me of the vision that appeared to the Apostle Paul of a man of Macedonia who said, *"Come over into Macedonia, and help us"* (Acts 16:9 KJV). Even though I was busy locally, I had to accept this call for help. We began laying the groundwork by gathering some men to serve as advisory board members and men who would volunteer to help at youth rallies. We began scheduling youth rallies and on November 10, 1961, we conducted our first Greater Elmira YFC rally in the grange hall in Horseheads, NY. I invited an old friend, Evangelist Jere Brubaker from Lancaster, PA, to be our speaker. From then on, we conducted youth rallies twice a month wherever we could get an auditorium. These were held on Friday evenings since I had the responsibilities of our regular Area YFC rallies every Saturday night in our local area.

The attendance at our Friday night Greater Elmira youth rallies was growing. At one of our earlier rallies at the Volunteers of America building in Elmira, we had shown the film *Wiretapper*. On May 11, 1962, a total of 410 people attended this program, and the local police became very alarmed when they saw so many teenagers flocking into that area of town and into the VOA building. Ten minutes before the program began, a police officer called for reinforcements because this was in an area of the city known for teenage gang activity. He rushed into the offices of the VOA building and wanted to know who was in charge of the activity. He was one very nervous cop. The VOA director pointed to me and told him that I was in charge. The policeman began to question me about what was happening. He asked if I had ever done anything like this before and if I needed help to control the crowd. I smiled and told him that everything was under control. He still seemed unsure and appeared very anxious that I was not more concerned. I again assured him that everything was under control. This gave me an opportunity to witness to him and tell him what this crowd was all about. I then suggested that maybe it would be good for him and his fellow officers to stay with us for the program just in case his services were needed. I actually wanted him to see how hundreds of teenagers could gather without getting into fights and destroying property, which was what he was expecting. I also wanted to be sure he was exposed to the Gospel message. He stayed long enough to see that there were no gang fights that night. Eight young people trust Christ as their Savior.

On Friday night, February 14, 1964, our special guest speaker for the Greater Elmira YFC rally was Redd Harper, better known as Mr. Texas, star of the Billy Graham film. There was a capacity crowd packed into the sanctuary of the Calvary Baptist Church in Horseheads. In the middle of the program, there was a very large bang that caused a slight stir among the crowd. Some of the church trustees and deacons went downstairs to see if there had been an explosion, but they couldn't locate anything. I was told that they later discovered that one of the wooden beams had cracked because of the weight from the large crowd.

On June 5, 1964, we officially organized Greater Elmira YFC with a kick-off banquet. By this time, we had organized and conducted a few YFC Bible Clubs. Many of the Elmira teenagers joined our local teens for our larger YFC activities such as summer camps, holiday teen conventions, etc. The Friday night GEYFC rallies were being held in many different places, including the Horseheads Grange Hall, Calvary Baptist Church in

Horseheads, the First Wesleyan Church in Elmira, and the Volunteers of America building in Elmira.

I continued to be very busy with our local YFC program. With the growth of the Greater Elmira YFC program, I needed help to meet all of the needs. In 1965, Jim Hockenberry was hired on a part-time basis to direct the Greater Elmira YFC activities. I was his mentor, and Jim was later hired as the first full-time director of Greater Elmira YFC. Several years later, Jim moved on to another ministry. At that time, I was tutoring two of our local young college graduates as YFC interns, and I encouraged one of them, Dick Shelford, to pray about becoming the director of GEYFC. Dick had grown up in our local YFC ministry and had recently graduated from Cornell University. I had the privilege of marrying Dick and his lovely wife, Connie Tuller. During his internship, Dick assisted me with the Greater Elmira YFC program, and in July 1970, Dick became the director. This was another ministry that God allowed us to organize and then turn over to one of our trainees.

GANG MEMBER SAVED

Souls were being saved through YFC, and it was exciting to see God work in the hearts of teenagers—even tough ones. The Gospel of Jesus Christ is powerful. It is *"the power (dynamite) of God unto salvation to all who believe"* (Romans 1:16 KJV). We just presented the Gospel and then let the Holy Spirit work in their hearts. One such teenager was a tall, good-looking high school senior called Skip. Skip had dark hair and penetrating eyes. He was very personable and very popular in his high school. Unfortunately, he got mixed up with the wrong crowd and joined a teen gang in Elmira. This association led him into drugs, which led him to stealing jewelry from a local jewelry store. Skip was invited to the Elmira YFC rally on February 16, 1962, by a Methodist lay leader from Millerton, Dave Scudder. The rally was held at the grange hall in Horseheads, and Mr. Ron Nash from Houghton College was the guest speaker. Another participant on the program that evening was Keith, a tall, handsome senior from Corning. Keith was an intelligent young man, neatly dressed and very articulate. He was one of our trained counselors and, as a Christian, he knew what he believed and why he believed it. He gave his personal testimony and eloquently expressed how his life was meaningless until he met Jesus Christ. The message and testimony that evening was used of God to bring conviction to Skip's heart. When the invitation to receive Christ was given, Skip was the first one to respond. He came down the middle aisle of that grange hall, and it was evident that he was searching for something.

Skip was directed into the counseling room where Mr. Nash and Keith spent at least an hour counseling with him. He had many questions and wanted real answers. He understood that he had sinned and disobeyed God and the law. He recognized that God sent His Son, Jesus Christ, to die on the cross to pay the penalty of his sins and that Jesus later rose from the dead, proving that He is God. Skip was ready to make a commitment. He prayed to God for forgiveness and, by faith, received Christ as his personal Savior. Skip knew that God had forgiven him, but now he still had many wrongs for which he had to seek forgiveness and pay restitution. He was greatly concerned about his safety when telling the gang leader that he was quitting the gang, but he knew in his heart that he could not continue with the gang and be a real Christian. A few days later, he wrote this letter to Mr. Nash, the YFC rally speaker:

Dear Mr. Nash,

I want to thank you. I'm writing this to you about midnight. I don't know whether to cry or to be happy. I know from now on that God rules my life and He's come through twice in 3 days. On Monday I got up in front of

60 kids in my class and gave a testimony. When I told them that in the past year I had stolen some cards and sweaters our class was selling, I thought I'd lost everything. I was so scared when I got up in front of that class. But all of a sudden the words started coming out as if someone had control of my mind and mouth. And sir, when I talked even the hoods kept still and listened.

When I got through and walked out of the room, the kids voted unanimous [sic] to keep me on as class chairman and they still want me to go to Washington on the class trip with them. And one of the kids got me a job so I could pay back the class and now I have more friends than ever before.

But enough. I know what you're waiting to hear and it happened tonight. I stood up to Ben [gang leader] and told what happened to me. He laughed and started a fight. I stood up and beat him and knocked him down. God was with me. Every time I hit him it was as though God was in each fist. But all of a sudden, something came over me when he was down on the ground. God made me reach out my hand and help him up. Even after all he did to me, he started walking away without saying a word. All of a sudden the guys wanted me to be their leader. But I told them I was through. I left them and caught up to Ben. We talked for about an hour and for the first time in his life he cried. He said the only reason he wouldn't let me out was he couldn't do it and still be a big shot with the guys. Sir, he's quitting the gang and going back to his parents in Alabama next week, to give life a new try.

Sir, I've written Keith, that boy in Corning the same letter tonight. If we all pray for Ben like you did for me (because of what it did for me) I know it'll help him.

God bless you for everything.
Jimmy

I continued working with Skip (Jimmy) as he sought to make restitution to so many. I went to his high school principal and explained that one of his students had found Christ as his Savior, and he wanted to return a bunch of library books that he had stolen. The principal looked startled. At about this time, Skip had given his testimony to his fellow classmates. Many were in shock and began to ask many questions. The principal asked me if I would spend a day at the school to counsel with any of the students who had questions about what happened to Skip and how they could have that kind of peace and forgiveness.

Skip asked me what he should do with the jewelry that he had stolen from a store in Elmira. I told him that he had to return it, but to be prepared to be arrested if the storeowner became upset. Skip met with the storeowner and returned the jewelry. He gave his testimony to the store owner, who was dumbfounded. He was very understanding and did not press charges.

I met with the FBI in a room at the Elmira post office to give information on the drug problem in which Skip was involved. Skip spent a couple of nights at Pastor Dave Scudder's house where he went through drug withdrawal. I also met with Skip's parents who were shocked to hear their son's story because they had no knowledge of his involvement in so many things. At the same time, we were able to help his younger brother who was headed in the same direction.

Skip traveled with me to our YFC clubs all over the area giving testimony of the saving power of the Gospel of Jesus Christ. His changed life was an outstanding witness and testimony. Some time later, he and his family moved out of the area, and, last I knew, Skip was preparing for college to study medicine.

YFC HIRES ASSISTANT

As the local YFC ministry grew, it became evident that additional help was needed. In 1962, we hired Dave Justice as a youth worker, and later a full-time secretary was added to the YFC staff. Now we needed more office space. YFC Board Member Bill Sutfin, owner of the Avoca Coal and Fuel Company, offered the second floor attic of his building on Main Street in Avoca to be the new YFC office. The YFC board and some volunteers renovated that second floor attic into three rooms which became our new offices.

God's blessings were upon our efforts as the ministry expanded, reaching more teenagers and providing more services for churches to utilize. Leadership training, Bible quizzing, personal evangelism classes, Bible studies, formal teen banquets, "funspirations," retreats, and camps were some of the teen activities. Attendance at weekly Saturday night youth rallies, attended by all ages, grew as they were held in high school auditoriums in Avoca, Naples, Jasper, and Savona. When Saturday conflicts occurred with the high school auditoriums, rallies were held in such places as the Middlesex Town Hall and the Penn Yan or Bath Grange Halls.

The weekly Saturday night youth rallies attracted crowds of several hundred people every week. I would start the rally program with real gusto by running across the stage and shouting, "It's Youth for Christ time," while Lois Dungan pounded the piano or organ keys to our rally theme song, "Christ For Me." Everyone would stand and sing—

Christ for me, yes, it's Christ for me.
He's my Savior, my Lord and King,
I'm so happy, I SHOUT and sing.

Christ for me, yes, it's Christ for me.
Every day, as I go my way,
It is Christ for me.

The singing was always enthusiastic and contagious, especially with Lois at the keyboard. Besides singing many choruses, the program also consisted of special music, Bible quizzing, crowd breakers, and a speaker or Christian movie. Selby Smith transported a Hammond spinet organ on the tailgate of his 1957 Plymouth every Saturday night. In the back of my Rambler station wagon we hauled a big YFC sign, books to be sold at the book table, a sound system, and electronic quiz seats that our Board Member Dick Price built for Bible quizzing. It was a lot of work setting up and taking down all of this equipment every Saturday night.

I needed help, so I recruited the volunteer services of a young man named John Hayes. John was a local teenager who had recently accepted Christ. He became my assistant on Saturday nights. He was a good worker, and I could trust him to do the work of setting up and tearing down the equipment. When John graduated from high school and went to college to prepare for the Lord's work, I found another teenager who had recently trusted Christ. Terry Hughes became my assistant and rode with me to all of the rallies and did whatever I needed done. These boys were real laborers, and we enjoyed working together. Terry also went to college to prepare for the work of the Lord. They were just some of the results of our ministry with teenagers. Often, when we traveled the many miles to and from the Saturday night youth rallies, we had opportunities to chat and discuss the issues of life together. Little by little, their thinking was influenced by Christian life principles. They took their stand boldly for Christ among their high school peers.

REGIONAL RESPONSIBILITIES

The Lord's blessings upon this young ministry began to be recognized by other youth organizations. A few years after affiliating with the national organization of Youth for Christ International, I was appointed regional director for Western New York State. Along with my local responsibilities, we ministered to other YFC leaders by sharing ideas and know-how for becoming an effective ministry. At first I was hesitant to accept this position because I knew it would take some time away from my local responsibilities. Although it was an unpaid position, it was an honor to be chosen. I did not want it to become an ego trip, nor did I want the local YFC ministry to be hindered by these additional responsibilities.

Jackie and I prayed about this opportunity. I examined my motives and responsibilities, and I determined that this might be another door of ministry that God was opening. I came to the conclusion that everything I had and knew came from the Lord, and now I had a responsibility of sharing it with others. This would not take away from, but rather enlarge our ministry. I enjoy helping people with the lessons the Lord has taught me along the way. Nothing is original with me. It all comes from Him, so that is why He must have all of the glory.

BRAZIL

In 1964, Youth for Christ International asked me to lead a team of teenagers to minister in Brazil for two months. I considered this an honor, and the local board members gave their blessings. They continued giving me my salary and during my absence our club director, Dave Justice, took on the ministry responsibilities. Jackie and I discussed this opportunity, and I know Jackie had some fears and anxieties, but she supported me all the way because she believed this was God's plan. I had no idea how much I would miss her and the kids.

In February 1964, I was introduced to the team of five very talented teenagers made up of two girls and three guys, who hailed from California, Pennsylvania, and Illinois. We met at the YFC headquarters in Wheaton, Illinois, where we got acquainted with each other and formulated a music program. This YFC Teen Team sang together and presented instrumental solos on the trumpet, violin and the accordion. We also learned a few songs in Portuguese, which is the native language of Brazil. My responsibilities were to see that they promptly met their schedules, to provide counsel as needed, to be a chaperone, and to help resolve any problems that came up. Before leaving the United States, we presented a few of our musical programs for some local YFC chapters, including my home YFC Chapter in Lancaster, PA.

With passports in hand and our goodbyes said, we boarded an airplane in New York to begin eight weeks of ministry in Brazil. It was my first flight overseas, and I was rather apprehensive, especially since the airplane did not appear to be in top condition. As I sat in my assigned seat awaiting takeoff, water began dripping on my head. The stewardess didn't seem concerned, so I just continued to use my handkerchief to wipe my head. This caused me a lot of personal anxiety and led me to pray more. The jet finally took off, and we were on our way, while the water continued to drip for a short time. Thankfully, God answered my prayers, and we finally arrived safely in Rio de Janeiro about eight hours later.

Some YFC missionaries met us at the airport and led us to our scheduled meetings for the next two months. These two months in Brazil were a wonderful experience, but they were not completely without problems. One girl was very proficient on the accordion and another girl very talented on the violin. Two of the boys joined the girls with vocal numbers while the third boy, a Brazilian by birth, was the speaker and translator for the group.

Traveling, working, eating, and living with five very talented kids day in and day out got old very fast. I had to deal with some big egos and work hard to keep them focused on our mission and a spirit of unity among the team members. The group presented musical programs and personal testimonies of their faith in Christ before high school assemblies, churches, and government officials. They also made radio and television appearances. Brazilian teenagers were excited to see American teenagers and questioned the team about life in America. We could always expect some questions about the Kennedy assassination which had occurred a year earlier.

Fortunately, we had an interpreter who helped me communicate with the natives. On one occasion, I was placed in a Brazilian home where no one understood English. The family of four was very kind and helpful. I spent twenty-four hours in this home, and I was never far from my translating dictionary. The mother wanted me to eat more than one serving at each meal time. I tried to be kind by telling her that I was on a diet. I looked up the word diet in the dictionary, and while showing that word to them, I pointed to myself. They just looked at each other and smiled. After I had retired to my bedroom, I heard them talking and laughing while repeating the word I had used. I knew they were talking about me, but I didn't have a clue what they were saying. Later a missionary informed me that the word I had used for "diet" was a word used only by women who are pregnant. Now I understood those mysterious smiles.

There was some political unrest while we were touring Brazil. Missionaries told us that the Communists were gaining power and that their future seemed uncertain. One morning we were scheduled to appear on a local radio station in Curitiba. When we arrived at the station, we were told that the government had taken over all programming that morning. Our program appearance was cancelled, and all forms of public transportation were shut down. We couldn't go anywhere. It was a frightening experience to see soldiers surrounding the banks with bayonets on the end of their rifles. We stayed off the streets in the event fighting was to break out.

It has been said that all of the miracles in the Bible began with a problem. Boy, did I ever have a problem being in a foreign country with five teenagers and in the middle of a political revolution. I received a call from YFCI President Sam Wolgomuth in Wheaton, Illinois, inquiring about our team. He had anxious parents calling him concerning the safety of their children. I felt a very heavy load of responsibility on my shoulders, but there was nothing I could do but to give it all to the Lord. It is so foolish to worry when we are helpless. The Lord so often reveals Himself in our helpless condition, and I really needed to learn this.

Fortunately, the political chaos lasted only a few days, and the Brazilian Government squelched the Communists' plans. The government discovered barns full of ammunition, new currency, and documents with the names of people to be destroyed when the Communists took control. One missionary told me that their names were on that list. In light of these experiences, I was very happy to return home when my two months were up. Jackie and the children met me at the Elmira/Corning airport, and what a beautiful reunion we had. I returned with an even stronger love for my Lord, my wife, my children, and my country.

Someone has said that an occupational hazard in being a successful youth worker is the enticement to move on to the greener pastures of bigger and more popular ministries. That temptation came to me shortly after returning from Brazil. One of the largest YFC programs in the eastern United States offered me the position of executive director. It was a larger ministry, larger salary, better benefits, larger staff, and great potential. It was an enviable opportunity, and I was asked to prayerfully consider making the move. I considered it only for a moment and then responded by telling them that the timing was not right. I explained to them that our local board of directors and friends had just paid my way to Brazil to lead a team of teenagers, in addition to paying my salary for the two months that I was away. I felt it was a matter of loyalty and integrity to refuse their kind and generous offer at that time.

They asked how long I thought I needed to remain until I felt my debt was repaid, and I responded that it would be at least a year. They could not wait that long, so their offer went to another person. I never regretted that decision because if I had taken that position, I never would have had the privilege of being a part of what Family Life Ministries is today. To God be ALL of the glory. He had a plan.

Several years later, it was my honor to be appointed Vice President of the Eastern Area of Youth for Christ International. Mr. Earl Schultz, Jr., a man whom I admired very much for his business and organizational skills, had just resigned as the Eastern Area YFC Vice President to move to a new position with YFC in the national office. I accepted the position with the understanding that I would not move but, rather, conduct the Vice President's work out of our local YFC office. I would continue in the local ministry but have added responsibilities as Vice President. This gave me an opportunity to minister to a larger group of YFC organizations. The Lord opened these doors, and I felt an obligation to share what the Lord gave me and taught me with other YFC leaders.

I have worked very hard to keep my ego in check since I have been so honored several times with awards from my YFC peers. My theme through the years has been "To God Be the Glory, Great Things HE Has Done." I could never forget the Bible verse my father often quoted to me as a child—"*Pride goeth before destruction and a haughty spirit before a fall*" (Proverbs 16:18 KJV). It has been exciting to serve on the national level with YFC, but my real interest and love is in the local ministry. I realize that nothing ever happens on the national scene without first happening on the local one.

KICKED OUT OF SCHOOL

In 1965, the YFC Organization faced a huge challenge. For eight years we had used several local high school auditoriums for our Saturday night youth rallies. We rented the facilities and had a very good relationship with the school authorities. We were witnessing many spiritual victories in the lives of teenagers, but the enemy of the Cross was not sitting idly by. He influenced one person to create a problem that had the potential to destroy the YFC ministry. This person filed a complaint with the Avoca Central School Board, complaining that the school auditorium was being rented for religious purposes. It was determined that the complaint came from a local liberal religious leader who did not appreciate our ministry. Two YFC board members were also members of the school board and sympathized with our plight. When they didn't take immediate action, the Department of Education in Albany informed them that they had to remove YFC Saturday night youth rallies from the school to avoid legal action.

The other schools that we used for Saturday night youth rallies informed us that they would have to take similar action if just one person from their school district filed a complaint. I saw the handwriting on the wall. At a time when prayer had already been declared illegal in schools and the strong sentiment of separation of church from state was gaining strength, it was only a matter of time before YFC would no longer have a neutral place to meet for youth rallies. It could have been the end of this ministry.

We began searching for auditoriums, meeting places, or other facilities to hold rallies. We did not pursue church facilities because many teens attending the rallies were unchurched and were reluctant to go into a church to attend YFC rallies. Also, there were no churches large enough to hold some of the large crowds that attended YFC programs. The only other option was to buy or build a building to meet our growing needs.

This was devastating at the time, but it was a blessing in disguise. If we had never been forced out of the school, we would never have experienced the joy of owning our own building or the growth and outreach of the total ministry. The person filing the complaint meant it for evil, but God meant it for good.

Faced with the greatest challenge of this young organization, I did not want to think of it as a problem but, rather, an opportunity to see this challenge overcome through a miracle. Someone once told me that if there are no insurmountable obstacles, there can be no miracles because miracles require impossibilities. Well, with no money nor land nor building, we certainly met the criteria of human impossibility and an insurmountable obstacle. So, I figured this made us candidates for a miracle. I have always believed in miracles, but I had never experienced so many miracles as I have in this YFC/FLM ministry. Family Life Ministries itself is a continuing miracle. To God be all the glory.

Originally, I was not interested in building a building for several reasons. We did not have any money to build, but we were always current with our regular operating expenses. I hate debt, and at this point, we owed no man anything. One of my pet peeves is churches that spend millions of dollars on a building that is only used once or twice a week. This is a poor investment of the Lord's resources and is contrary to common business sense. However, the ministry was expanding, and I began to see the need for a facility of our own or this ministry would slowly die. The board agonized over this decision, and I sought the Lord for His direction. We finally decided that we had no other choice but to build. So, we took a step of faith and began the search for land to build a youth center. In this way, we became a candidate for the first miracle.

THE MIRACLE OF LAND

After much searching for land, I decided a good location was on land owned by Fay and Norma Stewart of Kanona. It was situated along Campbell Creek Road and US Route 15 near Kanona, just north of Bath, NY, at the crossroads of the area in which YFC was ministering. The Stewarts had farmed this land for many years. I had no idea of the value of this location, but I decided that I would approach Mr. Stewart and tell him of our need for land to build a youth center. I asked him if he would be willing to sell some land to YFC. He asked me to get into his car because he had something he wanted to show me. He drove down the road and stopped in front of the exact parcel of land I had chosen. He said that he had heard YFC was looking for land, and that he and his wife had agreed that if YFC took care of the legal fees, they would give us that land.

I was elated. I was overjoyed. I was excited. I was dancing for joy. We didn't need any money to buy land! I couldn't wait to get home and share this good news with Jackie. She rejoiced with me, and we both thanked the Lord for this exciting gift and answer to prayer. After I thought more about this gift and tried to visualize what we would build and how, I realized that the tract of land the Stewarts were donating was not large enough. They had no idea of the size of the building we were planning. So, I began to worry about how to approach them for more land. How do you ask a man for more when he has just given you a large gift? I worried about this for several days and then decided to pray about it. That's the course of action I usually take on matters like this—worry and then pray. I prayed for wisdom on how to approach them, and I prayed that God would speak to their hearts and prepare them for my request.

A few days later, I made an appointment to visit Mr. and Mrs. Stewart. I really felt awkward and did not know how to begin. Should I say, "Thank you, but we need more"? That didn't sound right. So, in fear and trembling, I stopped by their house, and we began some small talk while I nervously searched for the right words. To my amazement, before I could say a word about the land, Mr. Stewart said, "I have been looking at our parking lot at church, and I never dreamed that it took so much room to park cars. You will need more land for parking, so how much more land do you think you will need?" I was dumbfounded. I was speechless. I know my mouth dropped open and my heart skipped a couple of beats before I answered him. I told him what I thought we would need, he agreed with my assessment, and he gave us the additional land. I had just witnessed another miracle, and my faith was greatly increased as I personally witnessed God answering our prayers and preparing the way before us. From this experience, I felt that God must have some great things in store for this small ministry. To God be the glory. He had a plan. I have learned that God is always there before we are.

I couldn't wait to tell the world what God was doing. Jackie voiced her confidence many times that there would be a youth center built at this location, and her faith and confidence was a great encouragement to me, but I was a little troubled a few days later when a man questioned the gift of this land. He told me that the land was only suitable for farmland because of its location in a flood area. What an excellent way to pop a guy's balloon of enthusiasm and excitement after receiving such a gift. Someone has said that if you are ever given a lemon, just make lemonade out of it. So I started doing some research and discovered that the only time this land was really flooded was back in 1935. Mr. Stewart told me that in the '35 flood, the water just came up to the crown of the road. Right then and there, I decided that we must haul enough fill in to keep the location of the building area at least one foot above the crown of the road. Was that going to be high enough? Many years later we would come to find out the answer.

After the Stewarts had donated the land, a Hornell businessman, Mr. Laverne Bender, heard of our building program and called me one day to say that he wanted to be a part of it. He offered to provide the funds to buy adjoining land for the athletic fields. With his gift, we had our land. Now our next project was to raise money to build. I had no idea of how to do this. In all of my schooling, I had never had a course in fund raising. Dr. Bob Jones always said, "You can borrow brains, but you cannot borrow character." So, once again, I began to borrow brains as I visited numerous organizations and talked with their leaders about methods to raise funds for a building project. We were given many ideas, and several ideas were presented and discussed with the board, but none of them seemed suitable for our situation.

I was so convinced that God had a plan for a YFC youth center that I made a promise to the board of directors that would later be put to the test. I promised that if they approved the construction of a youth center, I would not consider any other potential job offers until the building was completely paid for. The test came shortly after making this promise. The same large YFC organization which had approached me earlier returned to talk to me. Things had not worked out with the man they hired, so they came back to me again with another offer to head up their organization. For me, it was an easy decision. I just told them about the promise that I had made to our local board and explained that I had to keep my word. If I expected God's blessings, I had to be a man of integrity.

THE MIRACLE OF PROVISION

In my eyes, there was no easy way of raising money. I was forced once again to look to the Lord and ask Him for a plan. One time, while on my knees praying, an idea to raise building funds came to my mind. I waited and listened. The idea expanded, and I became excited about it. I grabbed a note pad, while still on my knees, and began writing it down. As I did, it all began to jell, and it really made a lot of sense to me. I shared it with the board of directors at our next meeting, and they liked it. It was just a simple plan that involved every board member recruiting seven men to make up a team. Each of the seven teams had a goal, and each member of that team had a personal goal. We began to implement the plan and ended up raising $80,000 in cash and three-year pledges. This idea or revelation came after I had prayed and while I was still on my knees. It is important to be still and to wait upon the Lord following our prayer time. Too often I talk to God and then get on with life, failing to wait and hear what God has to say. If we spent as much time on our knees after praying as we do praying, we would get more answers and direction, I'm sure. The Scripture says, *"They that wait upon the Lord shall renew their strength..."* (Isaiah 40:31 KJV), and, *"Be still and know that I am God"* (Psalm 46:10 KJV).

To be a good steward of all the money we were raising, I wanted to design a building and floor plan that was very functional. It would include several offices, a kitchen, a basketball court, restrooms and a stage. Though it looked small on paper, my first building design was, in actuality, an enormous building. I had big ideas, but when reality set in, we ended up using my fifth or sixth design, which was about one-fourth the size of my original plans.

With cash and pledges of $80,000 in hand, we began to make plans to build. Groundbreaking for the new 140' x 80' building was an exciting event. The program was conducted on the flat bed of an old farm wagon at the building site. Guests brought their own folding chairs, or they sat on blankets on the grass. We had New York State Assemblyman Charles Goodell, the Steuben County Sheriff, board members, and other dignitaries present at the site of the new youth center. The program consisted of some teenagers giving testimony, some comments from the dignitaries, and special music. Several board members and officials took the shovel and turned over the first spades of dirt. The air was filled with anticipation and excitement at what was happening.

The groundbreaking event hit the newspapers, and the public became more aware of our plans. YFC Board Member Ed

Schuchardt was a real motivator in the fund drive, and he helped to recruit volunteers to build the youth center. We were able to purchase many building supplies through his business, which resulted in substantial savings. We hired a local contractor, Mr. Ray Conklin of Avoca, to erect the shell of the youth center, and then we used mostly volunteer workers and YFC board members to complete the interior. Many of the ladies kindly collected and parted with thousands of S & H Green Stamp books which we used to purchase hundreds of steel folding chairs. The YFC board members had work bees at the Center. Harold Marmor was one board member who worked several days a week. Charlie Warden headed up the planting and landscaping of all the shrubbery around the building. It was a team effort all of the way.

In the process of erecting the building, we ran out of cash to pay the contractor to finish building the shell of the Center. We had pledges, but the contractor said that he couldn't eat pledges. We went to seven different banks for loans, but nothing was available since money was tight at that time. One banker said that if his best customer were to come in for a loan to build a cottage, he wouldn't give him one. We were in a quandary as to how to secure cash to complete the structure. We prayed, and then someone told me that they would withdraw and loan to us money from their bank savings account. I immediately jumped on this idea and began to ask others if they would make a loan to help cover the pledges. This idea spread until enough people loaned us the money needed to finish the building. Some loans were at 4% interest and others at no interest. One banker friend, Chuck Houser, jokingly told me that I played dirty pool. He commented that his bank not only lost a potential loan to us because he couldn't make it to us at that time, but they also lost some savings accounts. For us, it was a win-win situation. We secured enough loans to underwrite the pledges, and we were able to continue building.

In 1967, we moved into the original YFC Youth Center. It was exciting—our very own building. After many months of fund raising, planning, and construction, we finally made it. There was still much work to be done, but at least we could occupy the building. The first few youth rallies were held with strings of light bulbs strung across the gym for lighting and cement blocks with boards for seating. We had a portable generator in the back of the building to generate the electric needed for the light bulbs. During one of those first Saturday night rallies, everything went dark because someone forgot to fill the gas tank of the generator!

Our building fund goal was "Debt Free by Year Three." On our third anniversary, we conducted a Sunday afternoon program in the Center with my good friend Wes Aarum as our speaker. When it came time for the offering, we informed the audience of how the Lord had supplied our needs throughout this campaign and that we had no debt except to the people who loaned us money to finish the construction. We reminded them that our goal was "Debt Free by Year Three" and that this was "Year Three." We told them that if they would be generous, we could see another miracle take place. After praying, the ushers came with large buckets to collect the offering.

There was excitement and anticipation in the air as the board members began counting the results. As the counting continued, it appeared that we might be shy of what was needed and, out of the blue, one board member said that whatever the total, he would personally make up for what was needed to repay all loans. There were shouts of victory. Praise the Lord! The offering was just enough to pay back every loan our friends made to build the youth center. We were rejoicing and singing "To God Be the Glory, Great Things He Hath Done." I have always said, "To God be the glory for the great things He has done, the great things He is doing and for the great things He will continue to do as long as we walk with Him and give Him all the glory." It's amazing what can be accomplished when we are concerned only that the credit and glory be given to God. To God be ALL of the glory.

The building's design proved to be functional for all kinds of activities for youth. Roller skating was a very popular event which reached hundreds of unsaved youth every month. Preteen skates were held Saturday afternoons and family skates on Friday evenings. To promote family togetherness, teenagers were not allowed to skate at family skates unless they were accompanied by a parent or guardian. Basketball was also popular at the Center.

THE MIRACLE OF SALVATION

One day a young athlete dropped in because he heard that we had two hoops hanging on the walls. He was an avid basketball player in high school, and once he found he was allowed to shoot hoops at the center, he made regular visits to practice his basketball shots. I struck up a dialogue with this young man named Charlie. He was a likeable guy, good looking, with an athletic build and nice personality.

I began to pray for him and asked the Lord to open an opportunity for me to share the Gospel with him. Shortly afterward, a girl in his high school class was killed in an automobile accident, and he was troubled by her death. The next time he came to shoot hoops, I asked him if he knew where he would be spending eternity if he had died in that accident. I don't remember his answer, but it was not convincing. When he later asked me some questions, I explained God's plan of salvation forwards and backwards. I could see that he was hungry for some spiritual answers. I told him to think about what I shared with him and that when he was ready to turn from his past, with God's help, and trust Christ as his personal Savior, I would help him if he desired. Otherwise, he could just talk to the Lord and confess his need and receive Christ into his life as his personal Savior.

Charlie went home that day to think about his life and his future. After serving in the Air Force in Vietnam for a time,

Charlie once again returned to shoot hoops. While renewing our friendship, we continued our discussion of spiritual matters. One day when I arrived back at the office after lunch, Charlie was sitting in the front office waiting for me. I greeted him, and he said that he wanted to talk. I invited him to my office where he told me that he was ready to trust Christ. Wow! I saw in his eyes that he was ready to do business with God. I never saw someone as ready as he was to trust Christ as his Savior. We got on our knees in my office and Charlie prayed, asking God's forgiveness and asking to receive Jesus Christ as his Savior.

Charlie got up off his knees and has never been the same. His life changed, his language changed, and his future changed. That man is Charlie Alsheimer. Charlie now serves on the FLM Corporate Board of Directors. He is not only my dear friend, but he is like a son to me. He has become one of the top white-tailed deer photographers, writers, and hunters in North America. His photos have won numerous state and national photo contests. He has written and co-authored several books on the white-tailed deer and has numerous multimedia nature programs that he presents to churches, civic clubs, camps and public schools all across the country. Charlie has an outstanding and effective ministry with sportsmen and is being used by God to lead many men to Christ. He is another trophy of God's grace reached through the YFC ministry.

WHEN THE FLOOD WATERS ROSE

Our long-ago decision to buy land in a flood area was severely tested when the big flood of June 1972 arrived. It had already been raining for several days, saturating the ground and raising the water table, when Hurricane Agnes arrived. She decided to stay around for a while and dumped more water on the already soaked ground. I was just returning from New Jersey on YFC Vice-Presidential business when I stopped in Big Flats to check on some building plans for a home for boys we were developing in a response to my conviction that we could save "many lives from despair and delinquency" by providing a Christian home environment. Much to my surprise, the architect informed me that the Bath area was experiencing some high water.

I was quickly heading for the office in Kanona, just north of Bath, when I came upon a roadblock. The police warned me that there was high water and all kinds of flooding. Unable to get home, I went back to Painted Post to spend the night with my parents. Dad was pastor of the Faith Baptist Church in Gang Mills at the time. The next morning, after detouring around downed trees, mud slides, and washed out bridges and roads, I finally arrived at the railroad tracks that run by the YFC Center. That was as close as I could get to the building. Water was at the front door and all kinds of debris was scattered across the parking lot. The building was literally surrounded by water. It was like an island as the floodwaters gushed by on both sides. The garage that had been situated in a low spot on the other side of the parking lot was washed away. We later found its contents on the other end of the ball fields.

I decided to wade through the water and check for any damage. I opened the front door and found that, although the building was intact, just enough water had entered to make the floors a muddy mess. I was so grateful that we were spared any structural damage and grateful for the man who questioned the land location because of flooding possibilities. If it were not for his comments, we may never have hauled tons of fill in to raise the base of the building.

After the flood, we immediately went to work cleaning up the floors and ordering new carpeting. It was during this process that one of the secretaries noticed an extension cord under her desk. As she went to pick it up, it moved. She quickly noted, to her horror, that it was a snake. Screams echoed all over the building. Her discovery really livened up the whole office.

10

❦ ❦

LIFELINE MINISTRY

HELPING TROUBLED BOYS

IN 1968, WE HAD BEGUN to work with troubled boys in a program called Lifeline. I visited some local high school administrators and shared with them some of the ways that we wanted to help troubled boys. Then I asked for the names and addresses of their troublemakers. Some of the school principals smiled at me and asked if I were kidding. They usually had inquiries for the top students, but no one ever asked for the names of troublemakers.

We contacted these boys and their parents or guardians, explained our summer camp program to them, and offered them a free week at a camp. Since it was free and there would be a lot of fun and food, there was no problem in getting enough boys to fill our week at camp. Many parents or guardians were only too happy to have their kids gone for a week. These were junior high boys from different area schools. The camp was a very rural and rustic site near Alfred Station, New York. It consisted of an old house, a bunk house, lots of woods, and a pond at the end of a long road. The boys could yell and scream at the top of their voices and not disturb any neighbors.

We trained and prepared our counselors for dealing with these boys. There were three basic ingredients in our program. The first component was a strenuous recreational program. We ran the legs off the boys and even played games like American Eagle at one o'clock in the morning if the boys were rowdy or couldn't sleep. Secondly, they were served all the good food they could eat. Our chef, Bob Versal, baked bread and sticky buns and served three banquet meals daily plus snacks. The third and most important ingredient in the program was lots of TLC (tender loving care). The counselors were sharp, athletic, college men in their twenties who grew up in YFC programs during their high school days, and for several summers they gave a week to counsel at this Lifeline Camp. We had one counselor for every three boys. Each counselor became the boy's hero and gained great respect from the boys since it was their counselor who would hit the home runs, score the touch downs, and win ball games for their team. The counselors built strong relationships with their boys in just a few days.

The only "religious" thing that we did on the first day of camp was to give thanks for the food. As we sat down for our first meal, I asked them where the food came from. Their answer was "the grocery store." When asked where the grocery store got it, they said, "from the farmer" who grew it in the ground. When I asked them what made the food grow, they answered, "the sun and rain." When I asked who provided the sun and rain to make the food grow, they finally conceded that it was God. Then I said, "OK, let's bow our head and give thanks to God for the food."

With the short attention span of this type of boy, we only took ten to twelve minutes each morning for a devotional program. The devotional subjects were: *Who is God?*, *Who is Jesus Christ?*, *What is the Bible?*, and *How do God, Jesus Christ and the Bible relate to me?* On the last evening, we had a bonfire, and each of the counselors gave their personal testimony of their faith in Jesus Christ. The impact of these testimonies by the men whom the boys came to respect as their heroes was fantastic.

Many of the boys sought counseling late into the night, and many trusted Christ as their own Savior.

One summer presented a memorable experience for me, personally. Each year, our camp counselors met at the camp the night before we transported the boys to camp. We spent the evening planning and praying for wisdom and strength to reach out to these troubled boys during the next five days. The following day, parents would bring their boys to the YFC Center from which we would transport them to the campsite on our school bus. This year, as always, the parents or guardians dropped the boys off, said their goodbyes, and left. Over twenty boys had come from many different school districts, so very few of the kids knew each other. As they congregated in the parking lot waiting to get on the bus, I watched from my office window, trying to size up the group. Just by the way some of the boys were talking to each other, I noticed that there appeared to be some problems brewing.

Suddenly, a number of the boys pulled knives from their pockets. Fear sprang up in my heart when I considered what might be happening. As I looked around, I saw one boy with a large machete. To me, that machete appeared to be three times its normal size. The voices were getting louder as they bantered with each other. They appeared to be taking sides, and as their knives gleamed in the sunshine, it looked like a conflict was about to begin. I certainly didn't want any bloodshed. A very real concern was that I had to drive the busload of campers to the campsite without any adult assistance. All of the counselors were thirty miles away at camp waiting for us. The only other person at the center was the secretary, so I knew I had to take action.

I prayed for strength and courage and then walked out between the two groups. With my shoulders thrown back in an erect position, I yelled out like a Marine sergeant, "OK guys, it is time to head for camp. I want everyone to line up and, as you get on the bus, I want you to give me your knives. I will return them at the end of camp. Come on now, line up, and get on the bus!

Come on, let's go right now!" I knew it was a face down, and I was hoping that they would be the first to blink. To my amazement, they "blinked." They looked at this old sergeant and began falling in line and following my orders. I know I was shaking as I collected the knives. I gave those weapons to our secretary, jumped into the bus driver's seat, and started the bus. I had the boys wave to the secretary as we drove out of the YFC parking lot. The whole way to camp, I kept one eye on the highway and the other in my rear view mirror, watching the boys and hoping and praying that there would be no fights. We arrived at the camp without incident, and I thanked the Lord for safety in the bus, as well as on the highway.

The YFC office secretary had anxiously watched this whole ordeal and my performance with the boys and their knives. After we were on our way, she called the counselors and informed them of the incident with the knives and the type of campers that were headed their way. They were concerned that they were getting some real hard core kids, so they prayed extra hard while they waited. These kids were tough, or at least they tried to act tough. We had to confiscate cans of beer that one kid brought in his suitcase. Another guy brought some nude girlie magazines that he hid under his mattress. These kids were looking for answers but were not sure where to find them. We fed them, played with them, loved them, and shared with them how much God loved them and really cared for them. The Lord gave us a great week, and many spiritual victories were recorded in the lives of these boys. We conducted these camps for several years reaching many troubled boys.

After the summer Lifeline camps and during the school year, we had the boys come to the Youth Center weekly for recreation and Bible study. It was a time of fun, counseling, and discipling. But, many times, the pressures of their old environment would begin influencing them, and our weekly contact would begin to fade. My heart was heavy, and I thought, "If only we could provide a Christian home environment for these boys to experience on a 24-hour basis, we could save many lives from despair and delinquency."

NEW LIFE HOMES-SNELL FARM IS BORN

I had gotten the idea of a boy's home from the YFCI Lifeline program in Michigan. I began to pray for a facility where we could provide the Christian home we envisioned for troubled boys. We searched, and we prayed. We had no money for such a project, but we knew that if God was in it, it would happen. One day, a lady called me and said that she had some property that we could have for the boys' home. I went to see it and met with her a couple times, but something just didn't seem right. I was skeptical and just had an uneasy feeling in the pit of my stomach. It was not long before I discovered that she had motives different from mine. Several years later, her building burned to the ground. I often thanked the Lord for protecting me and this ministry from what could have been some great pitfalls.

YFC Board Member Levi Weaver suggested that we might be able to purchase the Snell Farm which was located about three miles from the Youth Center. The farmland was rented to area farmers, and the remaining Snell Brother, who was 85 years old, lived in the fifteen-room farmhouse alone.

I met with Mr. Snell and Mrs. Bill Sick, his niece and heir to the Snell Farm, to explain our interest in the property. They said that they were not interested in selling the farm since it had been in the family for nearly a century; however, they asked why we wanted it. I just poured out my heart's concern for troubled boys. I shared with them that the burden on my heart was to provide a facility and Christian home environment where Christian parenting would take place. I was anxious for these troubled boys to experience a real Christian home where love and respect for each member was always evident. Our goal was to teach troubled boys the 3 R's—Respect, Responsibility and Reliance upon God. After answering their questions and discussing it further, the Snell family asked me to return the next week to share more. I did not understand why as they were not interested in selling the farm, but God had a plan.

While we didn't have any money to buy a farm, I thought I would at least find out how much money was needed and then ask people to help us raise the necessary funds. We prayed much that week that God's will would be evident in this dream of a Christian home for troubled boys. The following week, I returned and again poured my heart out, describing my concern for troubled boys and how we could help them with a Christian environment. Mrs. Sick and her husband said, "We are interested in what you want to do. We checked out your organization and found you to be reputable people, and we believe in what you are trying to do. We would like to help you with this project. We want to give the 170-acre Snell Farm to Area YFC." I was speechless. I was stunned. My mouth dropped open. Serving the Lord can be full of surprises, and this certainly was another one. I asked them to repeat that statement just to be sure that I was not dreaming or misunderstanding them. Again, God had performed a miracle. The Lord went before us and prepared their hearts to accomplish His work. To God be all of the glory.

In the gifting of the Snell farm, they requested that we keep the Snell name. They also requested that an annual stipend be sent to Mrs. Sick for the remainder of her life and asked that a family member be allowed to attend board meetings. Mrs. Sick died several years later of cancer, and her husband attended our board meetings for several years before he went to a nursing home.

We immediately went to work in developing a child-care program. We wanted to provide a quality program and decided to follow the guidelines and standards suggested by the Department of Social Services. Larry Taylor, one of our YFC youth workers, had experience as a Probation Officer and began writing programs for working with troubled boys. Larry developed a procedures manual that exceeded Social Services' requirements. We received a lot of encouragement from local law enforcement people like Steuben County Sheriff Jack Lisi, as well as some judges and attorneys.

We shared the good news of the gift of the farm and our plan for a home for troubled boys with everyone. A brochure was sent to every mailing address in Steuben County. I presented the project to service clubs, churches, the county legislators, professional groups, and everyone else I could reach. Once again, we asked our friends to help us by making interest-free or low interest loans to help prepare the housing and other facilities. Through this generous assistance, we were able to build a new barn, vocational building, two new homes for boys, a school building, and remodel the farmhouse into offices and apartments.

Many volunteers worked diligently in preparing this facility. Levi Weaver, a local farmer and board member, provided many hours of labor with some of his heavy equipment in building a pond, a vocational building, a new barn, burying water lines, digging foundations, etc. The first house had six bedrooms and an apartment at the end of the building for the house parents and their family. One county judge was anxious for us to open as he was holding up a referral of a boy for our facility. We just completed the construction of the first house and had received our license to operate as a child care facility when we accepted our first boy in 1973. Larry Taylor became the director of the new program, known as New Life Homes-Snell Farm.

Tim and Julia Smith, who were YFC kids in high school, were hired as our first house parents. They moved into the apartment with their children in June of 1973. The house parents were assisted in the home by a single male college graduate called "Uncle." He helped supervise twelve boys, ages nine to twelve. These boys interacted with the children of the house parents, and we worked at being a family instead of an institution. A large round table with a big lazy susan in the middle occupied the dining room area, and the whole "family" ate their meals together. The boys were taught auto mechanics and gardening, as well as how to groom horses, raise calves, do body and fender work on automobiles, and many other subjects that interested them. Mr. Glenn Rockcastle, a retired shop teacher from Rochester, NY brought numerous woodworking machines to the Farm and taught the boys to build things such as bird houses. "Rockie," as he was affectionately called, was an inspiration to the boys.

Because the boys were all under 13 years of age, they were still very teachable and able to be molded. One boy came into our care at the request of his mother. She called me on the phone and asked if we would take her son because she could not control him. She said that she had sent him to his room, and he jumped out of the window onto her car parked below. Another came from a divorced home where he was not wanted. This boy, Bobby, became so attached to our house parents that he begged them to adopt him.

The NY Department of Social Services and NY State Division for Youth began referring boys to New Life Homes in 1973. Since some of the boys found it difficult to function in a regular school environment, we began an educational program at the Farm.

A TROUBLED BOY SAVED

One afternoon, I stopped in at the house and about ten boys ran to me and started pulling on my arm until I promised them that I would stay and visit with them. We all sat on the living room floor in a circle, and I began to tell them of how much God loves them. Love, genuine love, is what these boys needed. I continued to explain, in a dramatic way, how God sent His Son, Jesus Christ, to earth to take upon Himself our punishment for our sins and make it possible for us to go to heaven. When I said that God would forgive us regardless of what we may have done, even if it were committing murder, one of the boys flinched. It was very evident that my statement struck home with him.

Then I remembered that the social workers had told us that we would have problems with this particular boy because he had murdered one of his friends in a dispute. The social workers, counselors, and psychiatrists were at their wits end in how to deal with him because the boy clammed up and refused to talk when he was questioned. It was because they hadn't known what to do with him that they had sent him to us. Being very new at this type of ministry, we prayed long and hard about accepting a murderer, but then we realized that Jesus accepted all sinners. This boy never spoke to any of the other boys or the house parents about why he was sent to Snell Farm, while other boys freely discussed their problems with one another.

As I concluded my chat with those boys, I invited them to accept Jesus as their Savior and to ask Him for forgiveness of everything they did that was wrong. That very day, this boy prayed for forgiveness and invited Christ into his life. He spent about two years with us, and he turned out to be one of the best boys we ever had. Several years after his graduation from our Snell Farm program, we received glowing reports on his attitude and accomplishments from the farmer who hired him. He was another one of God's trophies.

Sometimes when a boy could not cope with his peers, the rules of the home, or pressures from his home situation, he would try to escape these problems by running away. From time to time, some of the boys would get disgruntled with the house parent and decide to run. Many of them would stop by my mother and dad's apartment located in the old Snell farmhouse, before leaving. Abe and Anna Snavely became Grandma and Grandpa to the boys. Often, my Dad could be seen sitting on a bale of hay, talking to a discouraged boy who was contemplating running away. Dad loved these boys, and they knew it. They also loved Mother's cookies. To this very day, some of the boys remember Grandma's homemade root beer and how one of the bottles exploded in the cellar.

One of the first boys we received had a bad temper and a difficult time making the adjustment from his home to Snell Farm. In one of his bad moods, he jumped on the farm tractor and headed for his home in Hornell over the back roads. My dad saw him going up the hill with the tractor and decided to go after him in his car. The boy wouldn't stop. He even sideswiped my dad's car. Finally, he drove the tractor into a field, parked it, and started crying. Dad was quick to console and comfort the boy, and the boy returned to the Farm.

THE JUDGE RULES

One day, the house parents saw one of the boys walking down the hill. They didn't know where he was going, so they considered him a run-away. They reported his absence to the police, who later found him and questioned him as to why he ran away. He told the authorities that the house parents were trying to make him into a "Jesus freak." He was referring to the Bible memory program that we encouraged boys to participate in. It was strictly a voluntary program, but the boys did receive rewards for every verse that they memorized. When the Probation Department heard this accusation, they immediately called me in for an explanation. They wanted nothing to do with an organization that was making "Jesus freaks" out of their clients. I appeared at the courthouse, and the director of the Probation Department accompanied me into the chambers of the Family Court. The judge questioned me about the Bible memory program and why we promote it. I assured him that it was not a requirement for the boys, but that it was good therapy.

The judge questioned the "therapy" part of Bible memorization and asked for an example. I mentioned that recently one of the boys came to me expressing his concern about his English exam. He said that he had studied hard and was also claiming the Bible verse he had memorized from Philippians 4:13, which reads, *"I can do all things through Christ who strengthens me"* (KJV). The judge looked at the probation director, said, "That sounds like good therapy to me," and the case was closed.

Because of risks associated with this type of work with troubled youth, in 1983, we decided to incorporate New Life Homes-Snell Farm as a charitable corporation separate from Family Life Ministries, Inc. At the request of Social Services, many programming and treatment changes began to take place, and the boys referred were older and more troubled. The Christian home philosophy was being replaced with treatment programs. House parents were being replaced with child care workers. After beginning this ministry and being the executive director for twenty years, I decided, in 1993, that it was time to turn the responsibilities over to someone else who could give more time and daily attention to the program. My time was being channeled more toward the developing and expanding ministries of Family Life Ministries, including the radio ministry.

11

❧ ❧

EXPANDING RESPONSIBILITIES

ALONG WITH OUR MINISTRY to youth, we were also involved in training youth workers. We added some college graduates as interns to our staff. Ralph Eastlack, now executive director of the Youth for Christ program in the Wellsville, NY area, was one who received training with us. Several other local boys who grew up in our YFC ministry joined our staff as interns or youth workers after they completed their college education. I found it most encouraging that we were not only evangelizing and discipling youth, we were also training leaders. God used this ministry to train and teach many young men and women who are now in the ministry or on the mission field serving the Lord. Someone has said that the sun never sets on this ministry because the fruits of Area YFC are literally all around the world. To God be the glory.

The successes of the YFC ministry led us into other areas of ministry. Additional staff was added to meet the demands of a growing organization. God blessed us with a wonderful group of talented, capable, and dedicated people to help carry on the different aspects of the ministry. After working with youth for a number of years, I came to the conclusion that if we were going to be successful with them, we needed to help some parents as well. With the divorce rate increasing and the family unit under attack, we decided to provide Christian family/marriage counseling as part of our adult ministry programs. FOCUS (Family Oriented Counseling and Unique Services) was born. Today we have FOCUS counselors who are ministering to many hurting people who need direction and Biblical counseling for their personal lives, their families, and their marriages. FOCUS also conducts workshops and seminars including divorce recovery workshops.

We also saw a large and growing need for ministering to single adults. Family Life Ministries developed the group called SALSA (Salt and Light Single Adults). The SALSA program includes picnics, retreats, conferences and other social times which provide spiritual challenges as well as time to fellowship and socialize with other singles.

Another adult ministry that has proven to be very successful is the Ladies Luncheons. Several times a year, a challenging speaker or musician is scheduled to minister to women. The luncheons provide an opportunity for ladies to bring their unsaved friends to hear the message of God's love. It is a great time to fellowship over some excellent food. At each of these luncheons, I look forward to giving a brief report of FLM's activities and seeing spiritual blessings and victories.

Family Life Ministries also began a luncheon for senior citizens in the area. Over a hundred seniors gather once a month during the school year for an inspirational program and good food. Many of these seniors also enjoy the special bus trips arranged by FLM. Trips to Sight and Sound in Lancaster, PA and the Southern Gospel Quartet convention in Louisville, Kentucky have been most popular.

Dinner concerts and dinner theater continue to be very popular among adults. Nearly every event is a sell out. We feed a maximum of five hundred people in one seating. To accommodate the crowds, dinner concerts are conducted on a Friday and

Saturday evening, with a total of one thousand people attending for the two nights. The dinner theaters usually are conducted on two weekends. The dramatic productions feature local actors, as well as FLM staff members. Hundreds of people travel many miles to enjoy the productions presented by the FLM Performing Arts Department.

As programs and staff increased through the years, we were rapidly running out of space at the Center. The front office, which was originally planned for three staff members, was now accommodating seven, along with the office machines. Another office was converted into three offices. My office doubled as the recording studio for our weekly radio broadcasts that were aired over local radio stations. It was definitely time to expand the office space and enlarge the gym/auditorium.

FINANCIAL NEEDS MET

Over the years we were able to put some money aside from the different programs and projects that we scheduled. We trained our staff to always plan and budget for a surplus or profit from each activity. Roller skating produced some profits. The Coke machines, the snack bar, ladies' luncheons, dinner concerts and every other activity was always planned for a surplus. We saved these profits for capital projects or necessary equipment purchases. When it came time to build an addition to the Center, we already had a sizeable interest-bearing savings account to help fund the project. In 1979, the new addition was completed. It contained additional offices, a print shop, radio room, recording studio, shower and locker rooms, and conference room. The cost for this addition was $255,000. Loans were needed to complete this project so once again, we asked our friends for loans. Our friends responded to the challenge and several years after the project was completed, the loans were repaid as requested. To God be the glory for yet another miracle of provision.

In all of the different building projects in nearly fifty years, the YFC/FLM Organization has never borrowed a dime from a bank. We have borrowed from God's people and have always repaid the loans in a timely fashion. All of these loans were promissory demand notes payable within a thirty day written notice. We always had some financial reserves in a savings account in the event an individual requested their loan be repaid earlier than expected. We were grateful for the good financial reputation we had in the community, and we guarded that reputation with our very soul. Any loans that were made were always for capital projects and never to cover everyday operating expenses.

From the very beginning of this ministry, I wanted to operate in such a way as to never beg people for money. I considered that begging for God's work lacked discipline, planning, common sense, and faith. It sent the wrong message to the non-Christian. Watching some ministries operating on a shoestring and always in a financial quandary was a total turn-off for me. I was here to work with youth and not "beg" for money. I believed that if God ordained this ministry, He would provide for it. If He wanted it to grow, it would grow with His blessings and provisions. If the people stopped supporting the ministry, then I was always ready to shut it down and look for another assignment. I always believed that one must be faithful in little things before bigger things would come. I always planned to have at least one month's operating budget in the bank after all bills were paid. That gave us a cushion in the event something unexpected came up. I know some people thought we were rich because we always seemed to have money and paid our bills on time. They never saw our balance sheet, and little did they know how small our checking account was. Instead, we were efficient with the monies entrusted to us.

I know I made my share of mistakes, but, in my heart, I was determined to do things right, especially when it came to money. I always considered every dollar given to this ministry as a sacred trust and felt that I was the custodian responsible before God in the use of that trust.

GOD HAS A SENSE OF HUMOR

Another responsibility that concerned me at this time in my life was my children's education, and through this God taught me to trust Him in personal and family matters as well. As our children were advancing in school, I began to have a concern about how we could help them with college. During their high school years, I had informed the kids that somehow we would pay for their first year of college. If they were college material and wanted to continue on, they would have to find some grants, loans, scholarships, or work. I was primarily concerned with how and where I could get the money to pay that first year for four kids. A YFC board member asked me how my kids were going to go to college. I didn't have an answer other than, "The Lord will provide." I wanted to trust the Lord, but at the same time, I felt my faith could be strengthened if I saw some dollars somewhere in the near future. I really prayed about it.

One day, this board member arrived at my door step, handed me an envelope, and said, "This is for your kids' education, and when they are ready for college, you should be ready to use this." I opened the envelope and found a certificate for one hundred shares of Pan American Airways stock. I was overwhelmed with joy and quickly told Jackie. We rejoiced and thanked the Lord for the physical evidence of what we believed God would do when the right time arrived. I believe the Lord allows such things to keep us encouraged from time to time in this journey of life.

A couple of years rolled by, and Carol Ann was the first to head for college. I had been watching this stock for some time, and it seemed to be going in the wrong direction. The man who gave me the stock encouraged me to hang on because, he said, "It should take off sooner or later—after all, it's an airline stock." By the time Carol Ann was ready for college, my airline stock had fallen victim to airline bankruptcy. As I contemplated what went wrong, I realized that God must be smiling in Heaven. One of His servants had put his trust in this airline stock to meet the college costs, while He had other plans. God does have a sense of humor. In one way or another, we were able to pay Carol Ann's first year of college expenses, after which she was hired by the University's administrative staff. Later, she acquired her college degree.

By the time she finished her first year, Rick was ready for college. The first year's expenses were not as costly to me, personally, since Rick won a Democrat and Chronicle newspaper boy scholarship. He then paid the rest of his college expenses by selling books in the summer months and by working as a dormitory resident assistant at the University. Randy funded his college education through working at McDonalds and other jobs over several years' time. Ron completed his college education through odd jobs, working as a dormitory resident assistant, and traveling as the leader of a music group representing his college.

My Dad often said, "Where there is a will, there is a way." I am convinced that when there is a determined will and faith in God, mountains can be moved. *"I can do all things through Christ who strengthens me."* In some wonderful way, all of the kids completed college debt free. He provided for those college costs and often just in the nick of time. Oh, me of little faith.

WHEELER PROPERTY

In the early days of the Area YFC ministry, Ruth Foster, a schoolteacher at the Wayland Central School, had called and asked if I would speak to her home economics class on the family. I accepted the invitation and had an enjoyable time with her class. It was the first time I met this school teacher, and it was the last contact we had until many years later when I met her one day at the Steuben County Fair in Bath. By this time, she had to be in her 80's. I was walking by a food concession stand when this woman came right up and stood face to face in front of me. With her hands on her hips, and in her straightforward way, she asked, "Do you know who I am?" She caught me by surprise. I looked at this rather assertive woman with thick glasses as she stared at me, and suddenly I recognized her. I assured her that I did recognize her, and then she asked, "Well, why don't you ever come to see me?" I was again surprised and really did not know how to respond. I had had no contact with this lady for many years, plus I did not know where she lived. I said, "I didn't know that I was supposed to come to see you, but I would be glad to visit you if you so desire." She responded with a snappy, "Well you better come because I have you in my will." I assured her that I would look forward to visiting with her soon.

I had never had a confrontation like this before. I set up an appointment with her and did visit her and her husband on their farm in Wheeler within the next few days. When I arrived at the front door of their farmhouse, she opened the door and invited me in. She showed me to a chair and, before I was seated, she held out her will for me to take and said, "Here, tell me what to do with my money." I was never asked that question before, so I was a little leery. The thought that entered my mind was that this may be a test or trap. We certainly had many places in YFC for some money, but I was not about to put myself or the ministry in an unethical position. I did not take her will. I told her that I would not tell her what to do with her money but, perhaps, I could share with her ways that she might be able to set up her estate to save on taxes. Then she introduced me to her elderly husband whom she had married a few years earlier after the death of her first husband. During our visit, he was not involved in any conversation but sat in a corner of the room with his head bobbing up and down, appearing to be sleeping. During our visit, Ruth asked me several more times what to do with her money. When I told her that it was her money, and I would not tell her what to do with it, all of a sudden her husband lifted his head and spoke up. He said, "That's not what the priest would tell her!" Wow! And I had thought all along that elderly man was sleeping. He was paying more attention than I ever realized.

We had a nice visit, and I shared with her the Gospel and the many programs we have for teenagers. Before leaving, she asked that I visit them again. On the way home, I thought this contact would have been a fundraiser's dream. I did not get any money for YFC that evening. I did not think it appropriate to ask for money. It was a social visit, and I had an opportunity to share with them what the Lord was doing through the YFC ministry. I believed that the Lord would speak to their hearts if we were to receive money from them. I had come to realize from God's prior provisions, that if we are faithful in little things He will give us bigger things.

Some time later, I heard that Ruth had sold her farm and moved to a house that she owned across the road. She attended some of the activities at the Youth Center, where I saw her from time to time. She called me one day and asked if we could use a rubber raft at New Life Homes-Snell Farm for the boys. She bought the raft from a TV auction and put it in the pond on her farm. She put her ninety-year-old husband in the raft, and he nearly drowned when he fell overboard, so she wanted to get rid of it. I said, "Ruth, I thought you sold your farm." She said, "Yes, I did, but I kept about eighty acres of beautiful woods. We have picnics by the pond and it is a beautiful site."

As she was describing those eighty acres, I thought, "Would this be the site for the retreat center we were praying about?" For many months we had been praying and searching for a location to develop a retreat center. We set some parameters about a location. First, the site must be within ten miles of the YFC offices. Secondly, the site must have a creek or pond. Last, the site must have a lot of trees. With these guidelines set, we began to pray about a location. Without my knowledge, one staff member asked a real estate firm to help us locate some land, and when I found out, I cautioned the staff member that we did not need outside help on this matter. It was not a pressing need, and if the Lord wanted us to have such a parcel of land, He would provide it. Sometimes I get impatient, and think I must help the Lord answer my prayer requests. This is a formula for disaster.

We prayed for many months and looked at several properties, but none met all three guidelines that we had established. But, when Ruth called about donating the rubber raft and began describing her property, I knew it met our criteria. It was only six miles from the YFC Youth Center. It had a pond and lots of trees. Could this be it? So, when she finished telling me about these 80 acres she still owned, I asked her if she wanted to sell it. I explained what we were looking for, and her property seemed to meet our need. She said, "Well, how do you know you want to buy this? You've never even seen it. Why don't you come up, and I'll show it to you." I told her that I would be there in a few minutes.

I called Harry Ballas, director of the Snell Farm, and asked him to go along to look at this property. We jumped in my car and drove to Wheeler. Ruth and her husband were waiting, and she ordered me to get in her car and told her husband to get in the back seat with Harry. We started out of the driveway, and I yelled "Stop!" as she nearly pulled out in front of a speeding automobile on Route 53. She looked at me with a stern look and informed me, in no uncertain terms, that she was driving that automobile and she knew what she was doing. I felt like a scolded dog with his tail between his legs as I apologized and agreed that she was the driver. She was funny, and I know she enjoyed putting me in my place. That must have been the old school teacher in her. I later learned that her bark is worse than her bite.

We drove up through the wooded area of her property. As she drove, looking all around and telling me different things about the property, I suddenly noticed we were headed straight for a big tree. I tried to hold my tongue, but it was evident we were going to collide with this tree, and I yelled. She slammed on the brakes, looked at me, and said, "Do you want to drive?" I saw a little smile on her face that she was trying to disguise, and I'm sure she must have been chuckling under her breath. She finally got us to the top of the hill and parked beside the pond.

What a beautiful site. It was gorgeous—breathtaking. Fish were jumping out of the water in the pond. There were signs of deer. Next to the pond there was a large clearing in the wooded area where they had campfires and picnics. I began to dream. I asked, "Lord, is this it?" Finally Ruth asked me what I thought. I told her that this is exactly what we were looking for. Now, two questions—"Will you sell it?" and "For how much?" She looked at her husband and then looked back to me and said, "My mother was 85 when she died and I am almost there. I really don't need any money other than money to put clothes on his back (referring to her husband). I told her to think and pray about it before making her decision.

A short time later, her husband suffered a stroke and heart attack. I visited him in the Ira Davenport Hospital in Bath, but I don't think he ever recognized me. He died soon after. After the funeral, Ruth called me to say that she was donating the 74 acres of wooded land to YFC. Wow! Once again I was speechless. The Lord had touched her heart, and she freely gave the portion of the farm that she had kept for herself because of its beauty. Once again, I never asked for a donation, but God provided. Later she told me that the main reason she was giving the land to YFC was because her husband had encouraged her to do so. And I thought this old man was sleeping. No, I believe it was a real test and I thank God for giving me the wisdom to pass it. I'm just an ordinary guy serving an extraordinary God. Praise the Lord!

There were six acres of tillable land next to the wooded area that Ruth had for sale. I thought it would be wise to own this road frontage on Route 53, so YFC bought this additional land from Ruth, which made the total site eighty acres. We developed the site plans and building plans for a retreat center on the Wheeler property. We were preparing to raise funds for this project until things developed with the LeTourneau Christian Camp during this same time. The Wheeler property development was put on hold but has been used for camp-outs, picnics, and recreation by the YFC staff and youth.

LETOURNEAU CAMP

The LeTourneau Christian Camp—where I had served that memorable stint as substitute sports director after just arriving in Naples—is located on the east side of beautiful Canandaigua Lake, one of New York's Finger Lakes, just seven miles south of Canandaigua, NY. The Camp was named after R. G. LeTourneau, a Christian industrialist who provided the funding to build most of the buildings at the camp site in the 1930's. The facilities consist of cabins, a tabernacle seating roughly 200 people, a rustic dining hall and kitchen, a lodge, a bookstore, a recreation hall, a small house, and living facilities for staff. The cabins line the hillside above the old tabernacle. The view of the lake from the Hill Top residence is spectacular, and the 300 feet of waterfront boast a large dock used by swimmers and boaters alike. Water skiing and boating are just a few of the water activities at Le-Tourneau. Different churches and para-church organizations utilize the facilities during the year for camps, retreats and conferences. LeTourneau has a reputation for good programming and good food.

For several years, we combined our camp program with Rochester YFC camp. Another YFC ministry was organized a year later, located east of Rochester, called Eastgate YFC. Teens from this YFC chapter also joined the camping program until the three groups soon outgrew the camp facilities. Our YFC group, along with Eastgate YFC, formed our own camping program at LeTourneau. We called it AE YFC (Area and Eastgate YFC).

The summer camping program was a very effective and a large part of the YFC ministry. Many teenagers committed their lives to Christ during the week's activities. Not only was it an evangelistic tool where many kids came to know Christ as Savior, but it was a great ministry to Christian kids whose spiritual walk with Christ was deepened.

I quickly developed a friendship with the LeTourneau Camp director, Mr. Harold Seeley. He was a kind, gentle, soft-spoken man respected by everyone. He had been directing the facility since the 1940's. He had a heart for ministry, especially for young people. He had a very dedicated staff including two of his daughters and their husbands, Jack and Shirley Seabrook, and Otto and Edie Krein. Two single ladies who were just like family members were Avis Sowl and Jerry Moose. These people were like one big happy family, and they worked many years together, complementing each other and serving the Christian community.

Area YFC and Eastgate YFC co-sponsored a week of summer camp for several years. Two board members from each organization, along with the YFC directors made up the camp board. Tensions mounted one year as the Eastgate Director shared with me some philosophical disagreements that we had. He did not want the teens reading the New Amplified New Testament. He thought that version of the Bible was heresy. He opposed our suggestions for camp speakers. He was opposed to just about everything we suggested. At one of our camp board meetings, he became so upset and angry over a decision, that he bluntly told me and our two board members to pack up and go home. To his surprise, we did. We walked out, and that was the last AE YFC camp.

The next day I contacted Mr. Seeley and informed him of our decision to conduct our own week of camp that summer. He graciously gave me the dates and said it would be a pleasure to work with us.

I don't know what happened, but a week later, Mr. Seeley called me and apologized, saying that he had to break his commitment to me. He deeply regretted it, but he had to give those dates to Eastgate YFC. I never knew what pressure he must have received to retract his promise. He had no other dates available for that summer, so now I was under pressure to locate another facility for our camp. I was a little disturbed, but I later realized that God had to have a plan, and I just needed to wait upon Him. Mr. Seeley apologized over and over every time we met. He said that he wanted to work with us because he liked our group and he liked to have our large number of teenagers attending camp.

A few weeks after our decision to hold our own camp, two members of the Eastgate YFC board came to see me. They took me out to lunch and practically begged us to rejoin them for one more summer. They apologized for the way their director acted, and they asked us to overlook his actions. Their camp attendance was small and they needed our numbers. I prayerfully considered our decision and decided that it would be hypocritical and inconsistent for us to go back.

For over fifteen years, we conducted our week of YFC camp at different locations, including Watson Homestead near Coopers Plains, Odasaga Bible Conference in Arcade, and YMCA Camp Cory in Penn Yan. Finally, the Eastgate YFC organization came to an end and collapsed for lack of funds. Immediately, Mr. Seeley called me and invited us to bring our summer camp back to LeTourneau, which we did.

Years later, as we were developing plans for the Wheeler property, I received a call from Mr. Seeley that I shall never forget. He asked for an appointment to discuss an important matter with me. I had no idea what was on his mind. He came to my office and sat in the chair across from my desk and proceeded to tell me that he had directed the LeTourneau Christian Camp for many years and was ready to retire. He said "Dick, I am seventy years old and ready to retire. I have watched you and your family for over twenty-nine years and I like the way you operate and do business." I was astounded and gratified to hear such complimentary words coming from a man I highly respected and admired. He went on to say, "I have discussed this matter with our staff and board of directors and all are in agreement that if you and YFC would take the leadership responsibilities of LeTourneau Christian Camp, we will give the entire facility to Area YFC."

I nearly fell off my chair. I was dumbfounded. I was not sure that my hearing was functioning properly. I said, "Would you say that again?" He repeated it, and I was awestruck. I never would have thought of praying for anything that large. Here is the man who was forced years ago to turn us down for a week of camp that he wanted so badly for us to have, and now he was giving the whole facility to us. I had to pinch myself to make sure I was not dreaming. It really took a little time for the reality of this to sink in. I assured him that we would honor his confidence and generous gift to the best of our ability.

Upon approval of the Area YFC board, we began to take the necessary legal steps for the transfer of ownership. The appraiser valued the property at over one million dollars. There was no mortgage, and there was money in the bank. How ironic. The very facility that denied us a week for our summer camping program years ago was now owned by Area YFC. This was truly another miracle of God. God had a plan, and I liked it. We just had to wait upon the Lord.

"They that wait upon the Lord shall renew their strength; they shall mount up with wings like eagles; they shall run, and not be weary; and they shall walk and not faint" (Isaiah 40:31 KJV).

In 1986, the corporate structure of the Interstate Evangelistic Association, the official owner of LeTourneau Christian Camp on Canandaigua Lake, was dissolved, and all assets were turned over to Area YFC. We agreed to continue managing and providing camp facilities for churches and Christian organizations for their individual programs.

A SHEPHERD'S RESPONSIBILITY

As the YFC youth ministry expanded to include programs for adults, it became apparent there was a need for a name change. The "Family Life Ministries" name was now more descriptive of the growing organization, so in October 1986, the new name was adopted. Family Life Ministries, Inc. is a not-for-profit 501(c)(3) charitable corporation registered with the Internal Revenue Service and New York State Bureau of Charitable Contributions. Along with the expanded ministries came the need for additional staff.

With the increasing numbers of staff members, I recognized that my responsibility as the executive director included the role of a shepherd. The board of directors was a group of godly men to whom I looked as my counselors. They gave me direction, encouragement, guidance, and prayer support as I, with God's help, motivated and directed the staff of over fifty people. I felt responsible to provide spiritual encouragement and direction for each member. Keeping harmony with so many talented and gifted people and keeping everyone pulling in the same direction was no easy task. This reminded me of my grandfather's team of mules when working in the fields. They all had to pull together and in step with each other to get the most horsepower. This probably was one of my most challenging jobs.

My philosophy in dealing with the staff has always been that "THE WORKER IS MORE IMPORTANT THAN THE WORK." Jesus Christ died for the worker, not the work. The most difficult decisions I have ever had to make have been over the dismissal of a staff member. Before I ever made that final decision, I tried to help the worker. I prayed much over that worker. I reminded myself that the worker is a child of God, and I must treat him or her as such. In one instance, I counseled, prayed over, prayed with, and did all that I knew how to help this person over a period of several years before finally dismissing them. In every instance, I was guided by this principle of the worker being more important than the work, but I came to the point where I sincerely believed that dismissing the worker was the best thing for the worker and the work. Each staff member is one of God's children. I do not own them, so I never refer to them as "my staff" or "my secretary" because they don't belong to me. They are entrusted to me to teach, train, and encourage to do the work of the Lord. They are special.

Guiding, motivating, and leading a Christian staff has its advantages and disadvantages. There is a fine line between a friend and a supervisor. As friends, we are on the same level, but when my friend becomes my supervisor, they have just been moved up a notch, and now I am accountable to him or her for my work. We can still be friends, but we have different responsibilities. Some Christian staff members expect certain privileges and favors from their supervisor simply because they both are Christians. That attitude destroys relationships.

As a supervisor of Christian workers, I found comfort and wisdom in praying for and with them for any concern they expressed. Often in my daily prayer times, I would begin naming those at the front office and go down the hall praying for each staff member and for wisdom in relating to them and helping them do their best for the glory of God. From time to time I would pop my head into an office or meet a staff member in the hall with the question "Are you glad that you're saved?" The immediate reactions were varied but it always reminded them of God's grace, mercy and love.

I recall dealing with a staff member who boldly lied when confronted with a situation. The maintenance man told me that someone had run over our water hose with the lawn mower and chewed it up. I confronted the staff member who was last seen using the mower. He stood in front of my desk and emphatically said that he did not do it. I asked him the second time and again he outright denied that he did it. I looked him straight in the eye and said, "I want you to look into my eyes and, for the third time, I am asking you, did you run over the garden hose with the lawn mower?" Again, he denied that he did. I thanked him for his time and wished him a good day. The following morning he came into my office, stood in front of my desk with his head bowed and apologized and confessed that he lied about running over that garden hose. I asked him why he had lied. He said that he was afraid that I would yell at him. When I asked him if I had ever yelled at him, he said, "No, but my former boss did." I prayed with him while he confessed his sin to God. I forgave him, and God forgave him as He promised He would in I John 1:9—*"If we confess our sins, He is faithful and just to forgive us our sins and to cleanse us from all unrighteousness"* (KJV).

Another incident of God's spirit working in a Christian staff member was when I shared a particular devotional with the staff at a weekly staff meeting. I spoke on honesty and integrity as we minister. I had no one in mind when I chose this topic, but God knew. The following day, a relatively new staff member came to me and said that she had taken some candy from the kitchen and was sorry. She wanted me to know that she placed some money in the empty cash register to pay back what she had taken. Later I checked the cash register and found a fifty dollar bill. Seeing results like this makes it a privilege to work with Christian staff. None of us is perfect because God is still working on us.

12

❧ ❧

FAMILY LIFE NETWORK

THE EARLY DAYS OF RADIO

IN 1969, LONG BEFORE we ever thought of operating a radio station, we actually did live broadcasting from the stage of the YFC Center. The local Bath radio station offered us a couple of hours of radio time every Saturday morning for several months and would allow us to do anything we wanted to do. When Bob Lent, one of our YFC kids heard about this offer, he wanted to be involved. Bob was a teenager and a very nervous and emotional character that was crazy about electronics. He said that he could hook up all of the mikes and turntables for our music, and make the telephone connections with the Bath station. He was confident that he could do whatever was necessary (or, at least, he acted confident). I was concerned that Bob's nervous energy would create all kinds of problems in the middle of a live broadcast if one little mishap were to occur, but, after some thought we decided to give it our best shot. Bob went to work stringing wires across the floor and setting up a makeshift radio studio on the stage. As we started our initial broadcast, Bob communicated with the station personnel in Bath via the telephone for his last minute instructions. He was the key man to make this happen, and if he fell apart emotionally we were off the air and out of business. I watched him make all kinds of facial expressions and bodily gestures while sweating profusely as he made the line connection with the Bath station's studio. As the nine a.m. hour approached, Bob grew more nervous. He was jumping up and down on his chair and making all kinds of hilarious facial and hand gestures to communicate to us that we were about to go on the air. It was a funny sight to behold.

There was nothing professional about our broadcasting. Since all mikes were live, we used all kinds of hand signals and gestures to communicate among ourselves as we filled up the hours of programming by broadcasting sports news, spinning records of Christian music, commenting on current events, and reading some short devotionals.

Our radio staff consisted of our two YFC interns, Dick Shelford and Dan Smith, who helped me with all of the programming. Dan Smith was our sports announcer and commentator. Dick commented on some current events and miscellaneous items garnered from the morning newspaper. He also announced upcoming YFC events. While supervising the programming, I filled in with some devotional thoughts, interviewed some Christian teenagers, and had a mini-talk show with the two YFC interns.

Bob Lent thoroughly enjoyed his title as chief engineer as he sat in his chair with a huge headset the size of large dinner platters. At the top of each hour, Bob would send the program back to the station in Bath for the station break and the news. He closely watched the big clock that we hung on the stage curtain. He would hold his hand up in the air and drop it like the start of the Indianapolis 500 race. That was our signal to begin talking. Every once in a while, Bob would bounce in his chair, throw his arms in the air, make all kinds of gestures, and sweat profusely. When this happened, we immediately knew something was wrong. Either we had lost communication with the station in

Bath, or some wire had come loose. Such were the early days of radio for YFC/FLM. God certainly does have a good sense of humor.

We spent several months actually broadcasting from the YFC Center, and this experience whetted my appetite for a Christian radio station. Mr. Gratton Taylor had just built an FM station in the Hammondsport, NY area, and I heard that he might be interested in selling it. I asked the Lord for wisdom and direction as I made a trip up to the Bully Hill Winery to meet Mr. Taylor. He showed me around his facilities, and I noted that the radio station was only a small part of them. He had many other projects and ideas that he was working on at that time and radio appeared to be merely an investment for him. After several follow-up telephone calls, it was evident that this was not going to work out. It was shortly afterwards that this FM frequency was moved from Hammondsport to Bath, NY. It was very evident that it was just not God's timing for YFC to expand its ministry into radio—that would come later.

Looking back, we really knew very little about the operation of a radio station, but that first opportunity to broadcast was fun and exciting. We had no way of knowing that this would be the beginning of Family Life's radio broadcasting and that it would develop into a network of radio stations broadcasting 24 hours a day, seven days a week, all across Western New York, northern Pennsylvania, and around the world via the Internet. God had some great plans, and He was just preparing us for those plans.

WCIK-BATH (Where Christ Is King)

The Saturday night YFC youth rallies were well attended at the YFC Center. We were able to present excellent programs using musicians, drama productions, etc., but I felt that we needed to share all of this talent with a wider audience. I began to think of ways in which we could share these exciting programs and, at the same time, share the Gospel with the community and let them know that we existed. I thought the best way would be to video-tape our programs and then take the taped programs to the local TV cable companies and have them televise it over their community cable systems. So, in 1978, I asked my son Rick to accompany me to the National Religious Broadcasters Convention in Washington, DC, where I planned to get some ideas on television equipment.

The NRB convention was awesome. Hundreds of vendors occupied thousands of square feet of floor space marketing their products. The products included anything that was even slightly related to radio and TV. It was fun and exciting to see the latest technology used in broadcasting the Gospel of Jesus Christ. I met some of my old YFC buddies who were in Christian radio at this convention, and they encouraged us to consider FM radio instead of TV.

One of my friends in radio suggested that I get a commercial radio frequency and set the radio station up in my name as my personal business. He said that it would provide me a nice retirement and leave something for my family. This suggestion did not appeal to me one bit. I was really embarrassed to even think about such a set-up. I was interested in ministering with radio— not making money for myself. I have witnessed too many Christians who used a ministry to get rich. I wanted nothing to do with anything that would dissipate my energies and time from reaching out to people with the Gospel of Jesus Christ. My life belongs to the King of Kings, and He is the one I serve. My retirement, if there ever is one, will be in God's hands. My desire was to use every legitimate means possible to reach as many people as possible with the Gospel.

Building a radio station was new to me, so once again I had to borrow brains. I have borrowed a lot of brains over the years. I began by asking one friend what I had to do to build a radio station. He said that we first needed to discover if there were any FM frequencies available for Bath, NY. It was 1979, and we were told that we probably would not find any, but we decided to go forward with a frequency search anyway. Our board of directors was concerned about the two or three hundred dollar cost for such a frequency search, knowing that this money would never be returned if nothing could be found. This was a lot of money to risk. The consulting engineer was certain that there were no frequencies available east of the Mississippi River, but, in his computer search, it was discovered that one channel could be made available for Bath, NY. The engineer was so surprised that he checked two more times to be certain there actually was an available frequency.

The next step was to prepare and file an application with the FCC for a construction permit to build an FM station on the 103.1 frequency that we found. The engineering cost to prepare this application was two thousand dollars. Again, this money was not refundable if the application was turned down by the FCC. This was a big step, and the board prayerfully and carefully considered it. It appeared that a door was opening to us and so, on faith, the board of directors voted to spend the money for engineering fees and apply for the frequency.

Since 103.1 FM was a commercial frequency, it was reasonable to expect that other parties might also file for this same frequency. Since we were likely to have competition, our engineer counseled us to make sure that we made our application as strong as possible. The two suggestions that he gave us for a strong application were as follows: 1. Appoint a minority as a board member. 2. Make every board member an employee of the station.

I knew that all of our YFC board members would not be working at the station, so we decided to form a separate corporation. YFC Radio, Inc. was incorporated as a non-for-profit corporation. To strengthen our FCC application, we only had three board members, and they all worked at the station. I was the president, my son Rick was vice president and my wife Jackie was Secretary/Treasurer. Jackie, being a female was our minority, thus meeting the first criteria for a strong application. Our chances for FCC approval looked brighter, and we were praying for wisdom and for an open door to a ministry in radio broadcasting.

We gave serious consideration in the beginning to being a commercial station. This would have involved setting up a sales force and selling commercials. The more we thought and prayed about it, the more we decided that the commercial approach would limit the quality in our Christian broadcasting. Also, we did not want to place ourselves in the position where money could become a motivating factor. Money is an important aspect to any ministry because it takes money to minister. But our priority truly was to minister. So, we decided to go by faith and to trust the Lord and our listeners to help us meet the financial needs. We wanted to be as professional as possible with quality programming, and being commercial free certainly added to the quality of programming. Too often, the Lord's work is done in a very haphazard and careless fashion, which is a poor testimony for Christ. Christian radio appealed to me only if it were done with integrity and first-class programming. I was determined that we would not beg for money nor accept any programs that did. If this were of God, He would speak to the hearts of His people to support it.

When we decided to go strictly as a listener supported station, it required that we conduct Sharathons to raise the funds for operational expenses. In the eyes of the FCC, the board of directors is the owner or custodian of a radio station. I was greatly concerned about this because I did not want people to think that they were giving money to the Snavely family. Since Rick, Jackie, and I made up the board of directors, soon after the station was established and in operation, we made some changes on the board of directors. I asked Jackie to resign, which she readily agreed to, and we added five other men to the board so that it could not be construed as a Snavely family affair. Later the radio board merged with the Family Life Ministries board to be one corporation with radio being one of the divisions. This removed all of the Snavelys from board positions and kept them as employees.

Our application for the 103.1 FM frequency for Bath, NY was not without its struggles. Because the owner of the local Bath radio station was not aware that we would operate as a listener supported, rather than commercial station, we received opposition from him. He was fearful that he would lose advertising dollars. His legal fees were a total waste, but his opposition did delay us for several years. We worked for nearly five years to get a construction permit from the FCC to build WCIK (Where Christ Is King) in Bath. Even though the manager and owner of the local Bath commercial station opposed our application and petitioned the FCC to reject our application, God had a plan, and our application was finally approved.

It was one happy day and I was one happy man when we received the notice from the FCC that we were granted a construction permit to build an FM radio station to be licensed for Bath, NY.

Excitement was in the air. We realized that we needed more building space for our studios and on-air room. We didn't have time to get an architect or building contractor, so Jim Travis, Rick Snavely, and other volunteers began working on a small addition to the building. This involved moving the septic tank—which was no small task. We dug ditches, helped to lay block, poured concrete, wired the rooms for electric and audio, painted walls, etc. We literally built the small addition at the rear of the building ourselves with some friends and volunteers helping us. It was a team effort, and everyone worked very hard.

Jim Travis became our chief engineer. He began securing equipment, seeking advice from other engineers, and developing the construction plans for this new radio station. Jim always loved electronics and took some college courses to prepare him for such a time as this. He was in his glory. Jim grew up in our Youth for Christ program and had been a typical teenager. Full of pranks back then, he was the guy to sit in the back row and create small disturbances at camp or rallies. I often looked at kids like him, thinking that if we could get that energy directed in the right direction, he would be a winner. It happened, and Jim became an integral part of Family Life Ministries and the Network.

The radio tower and equipment was costly, and we ran into that money problem again. I calculated that we needed $155,000 just to build the station and get us on the air. I reminded the Lord that this was His project and not mine. I was just an ordinary guy taking orders from the extraordinary God we serve, and now I needed some more money. So, once again we prayed and asked our friends to help us, and once again our friends came to our aid with contributions and interest-free or low interest loans to get the station on the air.

GOD PROVIDES

When the word got out of our need, I received a phone call from a dear senior citizen lady who asked how much more we needed to borrow to complete the station. I said, "Thirty or forty thousand dollars." "Well, make up your mind, what is it—thirty or forty?" the woman asked. I was tempted to go for the forty thousand, but I wanted to be honest with this dear lady, so after I did some fast figuring, I suggested that thirty would probably be sufficient. She told me to come and get it, and that there would be no interest on the loan. I jumped in my car and headed for Hornell where I met this lady and picked up a check for $30,000. I was one excited guy as I headed home with this big check, thanking the Lord all the way. I'm sure that people who passed me on the highway probably wondered what the big smile on my face was all about. I was just so confident that God was leading me all the way in this radio ministry.

After about three years, we had every loan repaid except that $30,000. Then I received the second phone call from this dear lady informing me that she wanted to take me out to lunch and that she was buying. She said, "Do you think your wife will get jealous?" She then added, "Well, she better not because I am old enough to be your grandmother." I assured her that it would be all right. I had learned long ago never to argue with ladies like this.

Over lunch at some greasy spoon snack bar, she said, "Do you remember that $30,000 that I loaned you?" I said, "I could never forget that loan." And then she said words so encouraging that I will never forget them. "Well, I don't want the $30,000 back. The reason is because I had seven grandchildren grow up in this organization, and I like to put my money where I can see these kinds of results." Once again, I stood in partial shock and amazement. I thanked her over and over again, and on the way home, I was rejoicing and again humbly singing, "To God be the glory, great things He is doing."

The FCC application required that our tower be located about five miles west of Bath, NY. We got the topographical map out and began the search for the highest elevation in that area. We found a site on the Dick Wilson farm in Towlesville. We discussed our plans with Mr. Wilson, and he was so gracious to allow us to build the tower in one corner of his field. One of the first things we had to do was pour concrete for anchors of the guy wires and for the foundation of the transmitter building.

We were tested, but we were so excited to get a radio station on the air that we were willing to go through high water, rain, mud, snow and any other obstacle thrown in our way. And we did. It rained and rained the day we planned to pour the concrete. The field was soaked and muddy, but we pushed on with our concrete plans. The trucks, loaded down with concrete, could not make it across the field to the tower site and sank down to their axels. This proved to be a serious matter considering they had a load of concrete that sooner or later had to be dumped somewhere. Our thanks again go to the Wilsons, who got their big farm tractors out and pulled the concrete trucks through the field to the tower site. It was a long day and a lot of hard work, but the mission was accomplished.

Mr. Wilson was gracious and kind to let us build the tower on his property, but as I thought of the future, I was concerned that the day might come when he might sell his farm. What problems would this create with the new owners who may not be sympathetic to our cause? What would we do if we had to remove the tower? The location of the tower is critical to meet FCC regulations, so we just couldn't find any hill and erect a tower. Since this tower site was on the edge of Mr. Wilson's land, I thought perhaps we could buy some of the adjacent land.

The adjacent property consisted of about five acres and a two story house. It was owned by Mrs. Bertha Jones, a widow who lived there alone. One day while I was visiting the tower site and taking pictures of the crew putting up the tower, I decided to visit Mrs. Jones. She was a Christian lady and was interested in our ministry. I told her that if she ever decided to sell her property to please notify me because YFC would be interested in purchasing it. She assured me that she would. This gave me a little security knowing that if something happened to the Wilson farm, we could still maintain this site by moving the tower a few feet over on to the Jones property.

It was only a few months after my visit that Mrs. Jones passed away. I contacted her son and told him about my conversation with his mother. He said that several people had already contacted him about purchasing the house and property. He also said that his mother had told him of our conversation and, because of that, he would give us first consideration. He said the sale price to us would be $18,000. The YFC board approved the purchase, and the deal was sealed.

After some time had passed, I received a request from Mr. Wilson asking for some financial help with taxes. Things were getting more difficult for many farmers in the area at this time. He suggested that if we could pay part of his taxes that were due, he would deed the tower site to us. The board of directors was in agreement, and the deal was closed. Shortly afterward, the Wilson farm was sold, but we still had the tower site. As the radio network grows, it may become necessary to erect another tower at this site. I am grateful that the Lord gave us some insight to plan ahead with the purchase of the Jones property where we can put another tower.

For several years, we also utilized the Jones house for some of our staff living quarters. We made some major improvements and rented it out when not used by our staff. In 2001, we sold the house but retained the five acres of vacant land.

Another provision that the God of Creation made for us was a clear path for our microwave signal from our studios outside Kanona to the tower site. This signal had to travel five miles from our studio at the Family Life Center to the tower in Towlesville without any obstructions. After cutting a couple of trees down next to our studios, we had a clear path for our signal. From my office, using binoculars, I could see the men on the tower installing the antenna. On the horizon I noticed a slight dip in the terrain which allowed for the clear path for the microwave signal. I am convinced that God, in His creation, allowed for this path in that hilly terrain for our signal. God had a plan—even before the foundation of the earth.

ON THE AIR

After nearly five years of working, wishing, waiting, and praying, the day of broadcasting finally arrived. On August 29, 1983, I arose around 5:00 a.m. much more nervous than other mornings. I quickly ate breakfast and headed for the office and radio studio. My son Rick and Jim Travis were there, and Jim was pretty confident that all systems were ready to go. Jim turned the transmitter on, and at 6:00 a.m., Engineer Travis opened the mikes and we began broadcasting. I cannot describe the very emotional event this was for me personally. I was so grateful to the Lord for His blessing of a dream that had come true. I walked down the dark hall of the offices weeping and thanking the Lord. We were now on the air broadcasting the message of Jesus Christ to people all across Steuben County. It was so exciting, and little did we know that this was just the beginning. God had a bigger plan.

After nine months of broadcasting, the operation began to run more smoothly, and now it was time to formally ask our listeners for their support. We scheduled our first Sharathon for May, hoping to raise $100,000 to cover our expenses for the next twelve months. The goal of 1984 frightened some of our friends. That was a lot of money, but we all began to pray for God to speak to His people and support this radio ministry. We knew next to nothing about conducting Sharathons, but just prayed and asked people to help us in this new venture. There was excitement in the air, as there has been with all of our Sharathons since, and it really climaxed at one minute after midnight on the last day when we exceeded our goal. We ended the Sharathon with the staff and volunteers giving thanks to our Heavenly Father and singing "To God Be the Glory, Great Things He Hath Done." A total of $102,065 for one year was raised. It is interesting to note that twenty-two years later the gifts at our annual Sharathon amounted to over $2,000,000, or over twenty times that first year's total. It is amazing at what great things God hath wrought. To God be ALL the glory, and to His people we give thanks.

A REAL SCARE

Late Friday afternoon the July 4th weekend in 1985, just two years after beginning this radio ministry, I received a disturbing telephone call from my daughter-in-law. She said that Rick was in excruciating pain, and she needed me to please try to do something to help. I immediately dropped everything, jumped into my car, and raced the two miles up to their house. Rick had seen a doctor in the past week or two for outbursts of this pain in his side, but he usually could walk it off. This episode was different. No regular medication could help, and the pain, which came every two minutes, was worsening. His doctor had already discovered a mass in his abdomen and told him that after the holidays, they would do more testing to discover the source of the pain.

I immediately called for the ambulance. Every time a pain hit him he would cry out in agony. Rick is a tough guy at 6'2" and weighing in at over 200 with broad shoulders. He could stand a lot of pain, so we all knew that this was very serious.

We asked the ambulance crew to take him to his doctor in Sayre, PA, where all of his medical records were located. Instead, they took him to the Hornell hospital to get him stabilized. Many doctors were vacationing, and the Hornell doctor that considered his case did not want to treat or operate on him because he did not have his medical records. After giving him some pain medication, we all headed to Robert Packer Hospital in Sayre.

By the time we arrived in Sayre, PA, the pain medication had worn off and Rick resumed his agonizing calls for help. Several interns examined him while we waited for his doctor. The doctor was away for the holiday weekend, and they decided to give him pain medication until someone was available to operate. It was so upsetting to hear this big man yell for help so the pain medication was most welcomed.

All day Saturday, he was on the pain medication. The nurse said that she had administered the largest dose of medication permitted, and it was larger than normal because of his size. By Saturday evening, his stomach had swollen so large that he looked like a pregnant woman with triplets ready to give birth. It was frightening, but there was still no decision to operate.

On Sunday morning, it was my turn to man the radio station from 6:00 a.m. until 1:00 p.m. Jackie and Sherri drove to the hospital to be with Rick. My heart was very anxious that whole morning. As I prayed and waited for news, I envisioned the Lord taking Rick home to be with Him. I could see our dreams of this radio ministry coming to a screeching stop. Finally, I committed Rick to the Lord and released him for God to have His way. It was when I let go, that I began to have peace that God was still in control and that *"all things work together for good to them that love God, to them who are called according to His purpose"* (Romans 8:28 KJV). I always knew this in my head, but now I had to live it.

Finally, I received a telephone call from Jackie. She and Sherri had been in Rick's room all morning, just waiting for someone to do something as Rick's bloated abdomen continued to swell. Finally, Jackie went to the nurse's station and demanded that a doctor be called immediately. Exploratory surgery was immediately scheduled for that afternoon. I was somewhat relieved but still anxious to see if God would spare his life to help me in this new radio ministry.

After my morning radio shift, I headed to the hospital and, later that day we met with the surgeon. He said that Rick's problem had been a blockage in the bowel. Tests revealed that it was not cancer, and I felt like we had just dodged a bullet. My first reaction was "Praise the Lord." Rick went on to experience a full recovery for which we all thanked the Lord. As I reminisce, I'm aware of my selfishness in wanting Rick to continue working with me and my lack of trust in God to work this for His good. Oh, me of little faith.

Our radio staff consisted of a few full-time people and several part-time staff and volunteers. Tom Nolte was our news director/announcer who was very committed to helping us sound as professional on the air as possible. In fact, Tom was planning to return to college when Rick became ill, and he willingly gave up a semester of college to assist us while Rick recovered. Tom's selfless attitude and help was greatly appreciated.

Our professionalism was not always evident. One time we had to remind a volunteer that he was playing a program tape backwards. Another morning, I awoke at 2:00 a.m. and noticed that our bathroom radio was not on. We always keep it on, but after checking the volume, I realized that the silence was dead air. I immediately called the station and received no answer. I waited and waited hoping that the young part-timer would realize that nothing was being broadcast. Finally, I decided to get dressed and run down to the radio studio in Kanona to see what was wrong. I had my car radio on for the four mile drive from Avoca, hoping that at any time I would hear music. When I arrived, I ran down the hall and, as I walked into the on-air studio, the part-time helper was just raising his head up from the desk. He had fallen asleep at the switch, and the music tape had ended.

WCIH-ELMIRA (Where Christ Is Honored)

Requests for a stronger WCIK signal came from friends in the Elmira, NY area. They wanted us to boost our power so that they could hear us better. The power for a radio station is determined by FCC regulations, and we were at our limit with WCIK. The solution to these requests was to build a station in the Elmira area. A key factor in building an FM station is to be able to find a high elevation in an area that does not interfere with adjacent stations. Our consulting engineer directed us to an area that the FCC would approve for a tower and transmitter. Our job was to find a spot with the highest elevation within that area. Jim Travis and I got the topographical maps, jumped into my car, prayed for God's guidance, and began driving and looking for such a place. We found the site in Coryland, near Gillett, PA. We concluded that it was probably a good site since another tower owned by a utility company was standing across the road. The site was owned by a retired farmer. I knocked on his front door and was greeted by his wife. They invited me in, and I explained our mission to them and told them all about Family Life Ministries and what we did. They were very cordial and easy to talk to.

I asked if they would sell one corner of a field that was not being cultivated. They thought that spot would be satisfactory to them, but they wanted to think about it. I left their home rejoicing and prayed that God would speak to their hearts if this was His plan.

The more these dear people thought about selling an acre or two, the more reluctant they became. If they wouldn't sell, we would have to start all over again in our search. One of their neighbors and a dear friend of FLM, Mr. Eugene Wilbur, went to bat for us and talked with the landowner to plead our case and cause. Finally, they agreed, and we filed an application for our second construction permit with the FCC.

After filing the application for an FM frequency at this site, the FCC informed us that we had to install lights on the tower, because of a nearby local private airport. This was an additional expense that we tried to avoid. The airport landing strip was no longer in use. The FCC would accept, as proof, signed papers from a certified pilot who declared the landing strip non-existent. Being a navy pilot in Vietnam and a prisoner of war, Mr. Wilbur was one person qualified to convince the FCC that the private airport indicated on the maps indeed no longer existed. That decision enabled us to build our tower without the special lighting. The Wilbur family also provided tractors and farm equipment in the construction of the tower. They were so helpful in getting WCIH on the air and helping to keep it on the air, and we are forever grateful to the Wilbur family for all they did to help us with this project.

WCID-FRIENDSHIP (Where Christ Is Declared)

We continued receiving many requests from listeners to boost our power signal so that they could pick up our station better. With the FCC controlling a station's power, we again decided to search for FM frequencies in these areas and build another station. One request came from Mrs. Jim Merriam in Friendship,

NY. Barb Merriam happened to come across a very weak signal one day on her radio. She knew it was a Christian station from the familiar music, and she liked what she heard. After listening for awhile, she discovered it was WCIK from Bath, NY. She contacted us and said that she and her husband Jim had a farm with a very high hill and that we could use some of their land if we were to build another radio station. She was anxious for her friends and others in their area to receive our programming. This was our invitation to Friendship, NY.

Praying, Jim Travis and I immediately grabbed the topographical maps, jumped in the car, and drove to Friendship to meet Jim and Barb Merriam. The Merriams are wonderful people who love the Lord. When we arrived at their farm, they took us up the road and into the field that had a very high elevation. They were willing to give us a choice piece of land for the radio tower. After consulting with our engineer, we discovered that an FM frequency was available at that location. We were excited and claimed Friendship as the next station to be built. After further studies, our consulting engineer told us that if we could find a location just south of the Merriam farm, our power could be increased considerably enabling us to reach many more people.

Once again Jim and I began a search, this time south of the Merriam Farm. Our consulting engineer made a circle on the topographical map indicating that any land within that circle would be satisfactory for our tower location for that 89.1 FM frequency. Jim and I traveled up and down roads, making several contacts with landowners. We finally thought we found the spot for the Friendship tower. It was located near Richburg, NY. I met with the landowner and explained our mission of constructing a Christian radio station in the area. I prayed in advance that the Lord would go before me and prepare this man's heart. After hearing my story, he was agreeable to sell us a lot for our tower. It was exciting to see the Lord go before me and prepare the way. God is always there before we are.

We had our share of Job's friends along the way—people ready to throw a wet blanket on our excitement in serving the Lord. We were advised by some people involved in Christian radio that it would not be wise to spend the money necessary to build this Christian FM station in Allegany County because it is the lowest income per capita in all of New York State. They advised us that we would not make it financially. We did not give this one serious moment of consideration because we are not in this ministry to make money, although we do know that it takes money to minister. We were confident that God was opening this door, so we moved ahead and bought the land and began construction of the radio tower.

Since the Station was licensed for Friendship, the FCC required that a studio must be located within the town of license. We just needed a place to set up a mike, tape recorder, and other communications equipment. We really didn't need this setup for broadcasting because we sent our radio signal via microwave from Bath, and later the FCC would grant a studio waiver that eliminated this requirement. For the time being, however, we needed some temporary studios within the village of Friendship to meet FCC regulations. I approached Friendship Village officials about renting a corner of one of their rooms for our temporary studio. Our request had to go before the town board and a public meeting. I attended the town board meeting one evening when our request was presented. It was interesting to hear some of the positive comments made by people in attendance who had heard of the Family Life Network. After some discussion, we were granted permission to rent a corner in the Town Hall for our temporary studio. It was only a few months before the FCC requirement was changed.

WCII-SPENCER (Where Christ Is Inspirational)

As the word about the Family Life Ministries radio programming was spreading across the Southern Tier of NY, requests began coming in for stations in other areas. We began looking at the Binghamton region. We realized that if we found a frequency for Binghamton, we would have numerous competing applications, especially if it were a commercial frequency. So we decided to look for a small, inconspicuous town where the FM signal would reach into the Binghamton area. That is the reason Spencer was chosen. Though the license would be for a small town, we could have a very powerful signal emanating from that tower site.

Once again, we were informed from engineering studies of the general area in which a tower would fit. Jim and I hit the road again in search of the proper elevation for the Spencer tower. I was the pilot and Jim was the navigator as we drove through mud and nearly impassable roads. Some of the roads were limited access roads, but we went as far as we could go. We found ourselves on one road that had ruts and sloppy, old fashioned mud three to four inches deep. We started up this muddy road determined to make it to the top of the hill where the map indicated a good site—if only we could get to it. I got part way up that hill and could not go any further. I opened my door and decided that I couldn't even walk in that stuff. If I were to take one step, my shoe would disappear. It was a losing battle, and I was not certain that I could even back down that muddy road. Slowly I plowed my way backwards with mud clinging to the underside of the chassis. We were not discouraged. We checked the map and discovered another way that Jim had indicated on the topographical map. We found it, and we discovered a telephone communications tower was already erected there, convincing us that this was probably the best spot in the area.

We met with much opposition from the Public Broadcasting Station in Binghamton when we filed applications to build the stations in Elmira and Spencer, NY. There was competition for the Spencer station, and consequently these applications were held up for many months. A petition to deny us the Spencer frequency was filed with the FCC by an individual in the Ithaca area. We had to hire the services of a FCC lawyer in Washington D.C. to fight for our cause. The lawyer spent many hours on this case and, at times, we were not certain of the outcome.

Our opponent told the FCC that we were not an educational entity and, therefore, we should not be awarded this 88.5 FM frequency. The FCC has set aside frequencies from 88.1 to 91.9 for non-commercial and educational organizations or institutions. The FCC asked us to prove our educational status. We petitioned our WCIK listeners, since it was our only station, to send us a letter within a few days if they thought we were educational. The response was overwhelming. We received over 1,000 letters in a few days. One man came to our office to personally deliver his letter. He was rather indignant and said that he was a listener and had learned much by listening to WCIK. He was so upset that our educational status was even being challenged that he used some swear words to emphasize his point. Perhaps he hadn't been a listener long enough! We compiled all of the letters, and our attorney presented them, along with his arguments, to the FCC. Shortly thereafter, we won the case and were awarded the frequency. We regard this as another miracle, because we had come very close to losing.

After several negotiations with the landowner, we bought the property for the tower and began construction. Several years later, a station to the north modified their station, allowing us to increase WCII's power and to move our tower site to the Owego area, closer to Binghamton. We later sold our original tower to New York State Electric and Gas Corp. and built a new tower near Owego on a farm owned by Mr. & Mrs. F. John Waite. They were so gracious to lease a spot on their farm for this new tower.

MIRACLE FUNDING

It was exciting to witness how the Lord provided the necessary finances to get the radio ministry off the ground. After repaying the loans for WCIK, our listeners provided the funds to build the Elmira station, which was not yet approved by the FCC. It normally took a year to receive FCC approval. We waited about a year before applying for the Spencer/Binghamton station because we needed the Elmira station to help raise money for the Spencer/Binghamton station. We continued to wait, but no FCC approval. During this time, there was the legal battle going on for the Spencer/Binghamton frequency. About another year went by and we decided to apply for the Friendship station. Now we had three applications on file with only enough money to build the one. I was rather frustrated because these applications were being held up. I was considering my plan, and little did I know that God had other plans… but, of course, He did.

Our FCC attorney in Washington D.C. had to deal with a competing applicant in Ithaca who desperately wanted the WCII frequency. This young man was working without an attorney and made some big legal mistakes that ruined his chances with the FCC. Our attorney told me later that if he had been the attorney for our competition, we would have lost, and there would be no WCII. Thank God for another miracle and another open door.

It was all at once that we received notice that the FCC had approved all three of our applications. Once an application is approved, the FCC gives an applicant eighteen months to build the station and begin broadcasting, and we had three stations to build with only enough money to build one. Our plan of financing the construction of these stations went out the window. We were planning on using one station to raise money to build the next station and that station to build the next one and so on. What would we do now? Where would the money come from? We didn't want to go to banks, and we hesitated to ask our

Christian friends for more loans. I worried about it and then prayed about it. I should know that when it is God's plan, it will have God's provision. How long will it be before I learn this? Sometimes I am a very slow in learning the lessons of life, but I thank God He is so patient with me.

Within a few days, and to my utter amazement, a dear friend came to my office with some good news. He said that he and his wife sold their home and property and were moving to Florida. He wanted to invest some of the Lord's money to help us build Christian radio stations. He and his wife loaned Family Life Ministries over $110,000 without interest. I had a hard time constraining myself as I praised the Lord. I broke out and sang "To God Be the Glory." That was all we needed for construction to get underway, and the Elmira, Spencer and Friendship stations were built in 1989.

A NETWORK IS BORN

A radio *network* was born on July 31, 1989 as the second station, WCIH (Elmira) was built. A few months later, WCID (Friendship) went on the air, followed by WCII (Spencer) a few weeks after that. We did not originally plan to be a network, but we continued to receive requests from people in the outlying areas to increase our signal. So, we looked for FM frequencies in their areas.

All of the programming of the Network originates in our studios in Bath, and we microwave this signal to the other stations. Since the FM and microwave signals are line of sight, we had to find a way to get over those high elevations near Almond and Western NY. This called for a relay tower that would take our Bath signal and send it on to the other stations. Once again, Jim and I got in my car, prayed, and headed for a high elevation where a tower could relay the signal. After a couple of trips and many miles, we located a spot near Birdsall in the Canaseraga area. We made a long term lease with the owner and began construction on a tower that would open Western NY State to future stations in the Family Life Network.

The uniqueness of the radio programming and the friendly announcers are key factors in the Network's wide appeal. We endeavor to connect with our listeners as one big happy family. To accomplish this goal, we sponsor concerts in our listening areas featuring popular musical groups. In this way, we meet thousands of listeners every year. Relationships are built when announcers meet listeners face to face in churches and other venues. A great attraction, especially for new listeners, has been the Morning Show which steers the listener toward laughter and a positive attitude at the beginning of the day. Jim Travis and Jay Johnson were among the first Morning Guys followed by John Owens and Denny Brownlee and the "Randy Man."

THREE MORE STATIONS

Once again, friends on the fringe area of our radio signals asked us to expand—this time into the Warsaw, NY area. When we found an available FM frequency in that area, Jim and I got in the car with our topographical maps, prayed for God's guidance, and once again headed for a high elevation. We discovered several towers already at one location, so it was fairly certain that there would be no zoning board opposition like we had run into at other locations. We contacted the land owner who farmed this land. He already had a tower on part of his land and seemed happy to lease us the land for our tower. When FCC approval was received, we immediately began building the Warsaw station in 1992. Once again, the funds came from friends of FLM who loaned us the money.

We traveled many miles in 1992, searching for a tower site for the Jamestown station. Our consulting engineer set parameters for locating a tower for the Jamestown frequency, and then we roamed the countryside within those parameters looking for a tower site. This tower had to be located southeast of Jamestown. After several trips to the Jamestown area, Jim and I finally found a spot near Frewsburg. We negotiated with a farmer who sold us a small piece of his land. Upon approval from the FCC, construction began, and within a few months, we were broadcasting from the Jamestown site. Since our signal to all of the stations was transmitted via microwave, we had to utilize three additional towers in order to get our signal from Bath to Jamestown. The first hop is from Bath to our relay tower in Birdsall, NY. From there, our signal travels to a tower in Freedom, NY and then, to a tower in Napoli, NY. Finally, the last hop is to our Jamestown tower in Frewsburg, NY.

There was legal work and the approval of zoning boards involved in all of the acquisitions of tower sites, but we never ran into difficult situations with zoning boards until we tried to buy a tower that was already erected in Bristol Springs for our Canandaigua station. The tower owner agreed to sell to us, and I filed the necessary papers and forms for the Bristol Springs zoning board. We figured that since there was a tower already there, it should be no problem to get permission to use it. For nearly six months I attended the Bristol Springs zoning board meetings endeavoring to get permission to use the tower that we intended to purchase. The zoning board said that the tower was located too close to the boundary line of the adjoining park and, if it ever fell over it would fall on the park property. I asked the park officials to investigate, and they wrote a letter indicating, that since this was a very remote area of the park and would not be affected by the tower, they would approve our purchase.

The park's approval was no longer acceptable, and the zoning board said that they couldn't give approval because the tower had been abandoned and, therefore, it must be dismantled. I checked with the tower owner, and he said that he had still been paying for electric at the tower. The zoning board assured me that if I could give evidence such as current electric bills to prove that the tower had not been abandoned, they would consider our application.

The following month, many area residents and supporters of the FLM Network crowded into the small town hall meeting room as I presented some current electric bills for that tower. Without even looking at the bills, they decided that this evidence was no longer sufficient. They kept changing the approval criteria from month to month until it became clear that permission would never be granted. I was frustrated. I knew God had a plan, but I wished He would hurry up and show it to me.

Jim suggested that we check out Bristol Mountain which would be a better site for a signal into Rochester, NY. Once again, we hit the road with a prayer in our hearts and a map in our hands to search for a tower site. It was a very foggy day, especially on top of that mountain. We drove as far as we could. We parked the car right in the middle of that path or driveway. The fog was so dense we could not see twenty feet in front of us. I was concerned about getting lost in the fog, but Jim seemed to know his way. We knew that according to the map, there had to be some towers in this area. All of a sudden, out of the fog, popped a tower site, then another.

We made contact with some tower owners and land owners, but nothing was for sale. Jim had a friend in Rochester who had a two-way radio business and a tower on that mountain. We were not certain that his tower would be strong enough for our equipment but, after investigating that concern, we made an agreement to lease a spot on his tower. Since that meager beginning with the Canandaigua station, we have made several adjustments, including a tower relocation that has enhanced our radio signal. Now we are sitting on top of the highest mountain in Western New York with our tower and a signal beaming out much farther than it would have from the original Bristol Springs site. God's plan was better. With our tower on top of Bristol Mountain, the higher elevation increased the size of our potential listening audience. On December 14, 1992, WCOT (Where Christ Offers Truth) in Jamestown, WCOU (Where Christ Offers Understanding) in Warsaw, and WCIY (Where Christ Is Yours) in Canandaigua were turned on within a half hour of each other. Chief engineer Jim Travis was running in all directions.

After building six radio stations in three years, it was time to concentrate on the need for more space at the main studios. We started construction on the rear of the Family Life Center to provide for offices, recording studios, news rooms, etc. The local planning board approved of the construction with the understanding that we would not build another structure at this location because of our location in the flood plain.

THE MIRACLE OF WCOG-GALETON (Where Christ Offers Grace)

A construction permit (CP) granted by the FCC is a valuable document which involves a lengthy application process. It is permission, granted by the FCC to a reputable and qualified person or organization, to build a radio station at a very specific location. Once an application is filed with the FCC for a CP, it can take approximately one year before the CP is granted or denied. Competitive applications for the same frequency can delay approval of a CP.

In the early part of 1996, I received a call from Bud Lefever from Coudersport, PA. Bud was a businessman, and he was inquiring if we could build a station around Galeton, PA. Many in his church were praying and were very interested in receiving our broadcasts. Because of this invitation and inquiry, we ordered a computer frequency search to see if any non-commercial FM radio frequencies were open for Galeton. The search proved to be negative, so we dropped the idea. However, Bud and his church continued to pray.

A few weeks later, I read an FCC report indicating that a commercial CP was granted to someone for a Galeton, PA station. I got excited and immediately called Bud to have him check the local library to see if the public inspection file was there. Such applications are usually filed at a public facility, so the Galeton library would be a good place to check. Sure enough, it was there. Bud was excited and called me with the information that I needed regarding the owner of this CP. It was a man from Du-Bois, PA, who already owned another station. He merely wanted to build the Galeton station to sell it and make some money. He would offer to sell it to us for $200,000 once it was built. He suggested that we give him a tax deductible receipt for $100,000 and then pay him for the other half.

Since the value of the station would be approximately $100,000, I informed him that I could not, in all honesty, give him such a receipt. I personally felt that it would be taking advantage of the privilege the IRS grants us to issue tax deductible receipts. So, he then planned to sell it to another company. I called Bud Lefever and shared the bad news. Bud was once again disappointed, but he and the church continued to pray.

Several months passed and, on July 6, 1996 I received a phone call from the owner of the construction permit for this new FM station in Galeton, PA. Since it was a commercial frequency, 100.7 on the radio dial, it was much more valuable than a non-commercial/educational frequency. He was inquiring if the Family Life Network was still interested in it. I told him that we might be interested in just the CP because we wanted to build it ourselves according to our quality specifications. He said that he would be willing to turn the CP over to us for $20,000, which was the amount he had invested in the application with legal and other fees. However, there was one catch. The FCC required that the station had to be built and on the air by July 29th—in only twenty-three days. If it couldn't be done, the CP was lost, since no more time extensions were possible.

Without a doubt, it would take a modern day miracle to build a radio station from scratch in only nineteen working days. It takes two or three months just to manufacture an antenna for the specific frequency that we needed. It takes weeks to manufacture a radio tower for the right height. It would not be humanly possible for all of the legal matters, the manufacturing of towers, antennas, and transmitter, and the installation of electric and telephone lines into the middle of a farmer's field to be accomplished in nineteen working days. There were just too many challenges to be met in that short time period. More miracles were needed.

I called my friend Bud Lefever and told him that we did have another opportunity for this Galeton station. Before I finished, he jumped in and said that he was not surprised because their church had never quit praying about it. They had been watching the proposed tower site and, since they had seen no construction activity underway, they knew that there may still be a possibility for the Family Life Network to acquire it. I told Bud there was a big "if" in this new proposal. We only had nineteen working days to build the station and get it on the air. Bud said, "We'll pray," and when he communicated this to his church, the Calvary Baptist Church of Galeton prayed—and we went to work.

I met with our chief engineer Jim Travis, and we plotted our course of action. Jim made phone calls to the equipment manufacturers regarding equipment that would be available for shipment within our time schedule. After reviewing this information, we decided, with God's help, to go for it. The tower manufacturer "just happened" (not a coincidence) to have a 199 foot tower in stock which would ordinarily take weeks to manufacture. The transmitter manufacturer said they could have a transmitter ready and shipped on time if we pre-paid it. We had an antenna in our storage building that was replaced when we moved one of our towers. The antenna manufacturer said that if we brought our used antenna to their Indiana factory by 7:30 Wednesday morning, they would have it retuned to the Galeton frequency by 5:00 p.m. that same day. This saved two months of manufacturing time. Jim Moore, our maintenance director at the time, loaded the antenna onto a trailer and traveled to Indiana. He delivered the antenna to the factory by 7:30 a.m. and, by 5:00 p.m. he was on his way back with the newly tuned antenna.

I called our attorney and asked him to prepare a purchase agreement for this construction permit. He immediately prepared the legal document and faxed the rough draft to me. I had to get the seller's signature and then file it with the FCC. At this time, the seller and I had never met face to face. We had only communicated via telephone. Our first meeting was in Galeton, PA when we viewed the proposed tower site and made some verbal agreements. Several days later, on July 11, I received the purchase agreement from our attorney and faxed a copy to the seller. For the sake of time, the seller and I reviewed the eighteen page legal document, word by word, over the telephone. After agreeing on some changes, I drove 1 3/4 hours to Galeton, and the seller drove from DuBois, PA, to sign the document. At the same time, I met with the farmer and his wife who owned the property where the tower was to be constructed. We needed their signatures on a lease for the tower site on their farm. It was critical for all parties to come to an agreement right away because time was running out. Jim informed me ahead of this meeting that he had made arrangements for concrete trucks to arrive the next morning. I felt the pressure of making this meeting a success in every way. I was praying and hoping that there would be no legal or technical glitches because everything hinged on getting the necessary signatures.

Our discussions were held in the kitchen of the farmer's house. The farmer, his wife, their son and daughter-in-law, the seller, and my wife Jackie and I were all in attendance. The daughter-in-law was a notary public and she notarized all signatures. Fortunately, everyone agreed on all aspects of the leases and contracts. Concrete trucks arrived the next morning, Friday, July 12th, just hours after we had finalized these agreements, and began pouring concrete for the tower construction.

While we had to wait for the concrete to cure during the next week, Jim was busy making plans and contacting people to expedite the erection of the tower, to construct the transmitter building, and to secure electric power and get telephone connections. At this point, everything was fitting together like a big puzzle in a timely manner.

At all of our other tower sites, we had constructed a transmitter building at the foot of the tower to house transmitter and microwave equipment, electrical and phone connections, and other necessary items for broadcasting. But, in this case, time was an important factor, and we did not have time to dig footers for the foundation of the 10' x 12' transmitter house, lay block, and construct the building. Jim suggested that we use a concrete building, the type used by the cellular telephone companies at their tower sites. With the clock ticking, finding such a building for immediate delivery seemed to be impossible. Fortunately, we located one that was a display model, and the company agreed to sell it to us. The building would be just six concrete slabs, the floor, the ceiling and four sides bolted together and sitting on sand on a level spot. Jim went ahead and ordered it.

On Thursday, July 18th, the tower arrived. The following day, the transmitter building arrived and was erected just in time to house the transmitter which arrived by express freight. The following day, our maintenance director returned from Indiana with the antenna. Jim Travis, Jeff Pfeiffer of Pfeiffer Electronics, the bulldozer and backhoe operator, and Bud Lefever all worked together to erect the tower, install the antenna, and make all of the necessary electrical connections. On Monday, July 22nd, the electric company had power at the site and, that very evening, Jim threw the switch to begin broadcasting over 100.7 FM in Galeton, PA. It was exactly 13 working days from the day we decided to build and one week before the FCC deadline. Wow! To God be the glory for the miracles He performed to make this a reality.

WCOV-CLYDE (Where Christ Offers Victory)

Jim Travis has always been in demand by other radio stations for engineering work. For several years, he did engineering work for Mr. George Souhan at his AM and FM radio stations in Seneca Falls, NY. Mr. Souhan took a liking to Jim and offered to sell his stations to him upon his retirement. Jim said that he was not interested in owning a station and suggested that perhaps Family Life Ministries might be interested. Mr. Souhan was interested in talking with Family Life regarding the sale of his stations.

A meeting was set, and Jim, Rick and I met with Mr. Souhan in Seneca Falls to discuss the purchase of his stations. It was the beginning of a good relationship. At this time, we were really more interested in a neighboring station licensed to Clyde because of its stronger signal in the areas we wanted to reach. Jim came up with the idea of buying the Seneca Falls stations and then selling the AM station and trading the FM station for the FM station in Clyde. The Clyde station owner was only too happy to have his competitor off the air as a commercial station and he would readily agree to the swap. We discussed this possibility, knowing that Mr. Souhan was not interested in selling his Seneca Falls stations to the Clyde owner, but he would sell to us. He said that he liked us and knew that if he sold to FLM, he would get his money. He said that he wanted to help us.

We did not want to mislead Mr. Souhan, so we were very honest and upfront with him about the idea of using his stations in a trade for the Clyde station. He did not have a problem with that and just said that he wanted to help us in whatever way he could.

A meeting was held at Miller's Restaurant in Penn Yan with Mr. Souhan and his accountant. After much discussion, we agreed to purchase the FM and AM Seneca Falls stations and real estate for $400,000. At the conclusion of our meeting, I stood up from the table and held out my hand to Mr. Souhan. He stood up, we shook hands, and the deal was finalized except for the legal work. On a couple occasions, while finalizing the legal work, Mr. Souhan's attorney questioned his client's generous agreement with us and wanted to make changes, but Mr. Souhan was quick to inform his attorney that he was standing by our original agreement. Mr. Souhan kept his word, and we kept ours. It is so encouraging to know that a handshake over a business deal can still finalize an agreement between two people.

The Clyde station owner offered to buy the Seneca Falls AM station from us for $100,000. He was also agreeable to an even trade of his Clyde FM station for the Seneca Falls FM station. We made the deal and ended up with the desired Clyde FM station plus the $100,000 for the AM station. We made the necessary arrangements with the FCC and, overnight, we began broadcasting Christian music, replacing the secular, rock and roll on the Clyde station. What a shock it must have been to the former listeners of the Clyde station when they turned on their radios on the morning of March 13, 2000, only to hear music and programming glorifying Jesus Christ.

We still owned the broadcast studios on Main Street in Seneca Falls, NY and all of the radio equipment. Instead of listing the real estate with a realtor, I put up some "For Sale" signs and, within a few weeks, we had a buyer at $50,000. So our actual price for the Clyde station was $250,000. We paid Mr. Souhan $50,000, and he agreed to receive annual payments of $50,000 with six percent interest. WCOV-FM in Clyde, NY began broadcasting on the Family Life Network in 2000, and we paid off the station in five years. I consider this another example of how God provides and continues to build this network.

FURTHER GROWTH

The radio ministry made a huge expansion in 2000 when we began broadcasting over the Internet. In 2001, we built our second Pennsylvania FM station located in Trout Run, WCIT (Where

Christ Is Truth). By 2002, the Family Life Network consisted of ten FM radio stations and twenty-six FM translators. The purchase of the Buffalo, NY translator provided a larger outreach than most of our other full-fledged stations. In 2004, a station was built in Arcade, NY—WCOF (Where Christ Offers Forgiveness)—which went on the air in December. Another station to be added later was Carbondale, PA—WCIG (Where Christ Is Glorified). During these past years, numerous stations received power increases, and additional translators were built. As Family Life Ministries, Inc. begins to celebrate its 50th anniversary in 2007, FLN can be heard in over fifty FM outlets across Western NY and Northern PA.

We have outgrown the present Family Life Center facility which houses the offices, radio studios, kitchen, Performing Arts Department, and auditorium/gym complex. In June of 2006, we purchased over sixty acres of land next to the Kanona Exit 37 off of I-86 where we plan to relocate as funds are made available. This new site takes us out of the flood zone and provides more visibility. Ultimately, it will house all of the facilities of the various ministries of Family Life Ministries, Inc. Growth continues to take place daily, so stay tuned!

13

❧ ❧

SAYING "GOODBYE"

TO DAD

I SHALL FOREVER BE GRATEFUL to God for the loving parents he gave me. I shudder to think where I would be or what I would be if it were not for Mother and Dad. They played a vital role in my life and ministry. Dad was a tremendous inspiration and encouragement by his example of how a real Christian lives. He was very vocal about his faith in Jesus Christ. He was not perfect, but he was an honest and moral man who had an unusual passion for Jesus Christ and the Word of God. Mother was a saint. She prayed, and she was by Dad's side all the way for all times. Mother and Dad made a wonderful home for my younger sister Marian, my younger brother Glenn, and me. It was a loving, caring, giving, and trusting family. I look forward to the time when we all will meet again in heaven. What a day that will be!

It was during the building of the Youth Center office addition that my Dad received some bad news. Both Mother and Dad were on their way to a family reunion of the Mellingers in Pennsylvania when Dad stopped by his doctor's office for a routine physical check up. He was in good spirits and feeling well and planned to spend only a short time with his doctor and then continue their trip to PA. Upon examining him, the doctor was concerned with his EKG and called for an ambulance. Dad said that he could drive to the hospital since he had just driven from Bath to Elmira. Since Dad had already had two heart attacks, the doctor insisted, and Dad was taken by ambulance to the Arnot Ogden Hospital in Elmira.

After Dad was admitted to the hospital, Mother called and informed me of all that had transpired. Dad didn't want her to call before things had settled because he said that he didn't want to alarm me. I went to the hospital and discovered that his angiogram revealed several blockages. The doctor made arrangements for Dad to be moved to Strong Memorial Hospital in Rochester for heart by-pass surgery that next week. I had never been down this road before, so I prayed, "Dear Lord, you are in control, so please give me the grace and strength to do and be all that You want me to be in these circumstances." I called my sister Marian in Anchorage, Alaska and my brother Glenn in Lancaster, PA, and gave them the message about Dad's upcoming surgery.

It was early November and just a couple of weeks before deer season. Dad and I loved to hunt deer, especially when we could hunt together. We spent many hours sitting in the woods engaged in "father and son" talk. They were special times that I shall never forget. As I stood at the foot of his hospital bed the night before his surgery, I knew that our deer hunting days were over. The surgeon explained the surgery and told us what to expect. It didn't sound good, but being the optimist that Dad was, he asked the surgeon how soon after the surgery he could head for Florida. He and Mother had spent the last two winters in Florida, where they had become very active in a Baptist church and its visitation program. Dad was a real soul winner and loved visitation.

The next day, our family gathered in the hospital waiting room while Dad was in surgery. It was a very emotional time of waiting. We would hear the good news and bad news of other's loved ones as we waited there. Now it was our turn to receive the surgeon's report as he entered the waiting room. He said that Dad came through the surgery in good shape, but the next few hours were critical. We waited, prayed, and waited. While I was walking down the hall, the interns were bringing Dad out of the operating room on a gurney and into ICU. I got a good look at him as they wheeled him by. The color in his face looked good, but it was quite a sight to see the tubes and ventilator and other paraphernalia attached to him. The next day, there were some complications, and those complications became real problems. He was hemorrhaging, and he was rushed back to the operating room where the surgeon reopened his chest to correct the bleeding. Again, he was brought back to ICU, and we waited and prayed.

I just grieved to see him suffering and unable to communicate with me because of the large tube down his throat. For one week, we traveled seventy miles and back each day to see Dad and to comfort Mother who was staying in Rochester with her granddaughter.

It was Saturday, one week after the surgery, when I was up in the woods checking out my deer stand on Charlie Alsheimer's farm. Charlie, my dear friend and brother in the Lord, was so gracious to let me hunt on his property. Charlie has always had a special place in my heart. This particular day was warm and sunny, and I lay down on a pile of leaves close to my deer stand. I just poured my heart out to the Lord concerning Dad. I knew we would not be hunting together this year, but I didn't want to lose him. I looked to him for counsel in many decisions that I had to make. He was my friend and counselor—the greatest influence in my life.

I felt a tremendous load and had a very heavy heart for my Dad and for the stress that my godly mother was experiencing. There was nothing I could do but commit them to the Lord. I asked the Lord for some encouragement and help at this time.

While lying there on those leaves, thinking of Dad and his physical condition, I heard rustling of leaves, and then I saw two doe walking up the side of the hill directly toward me. I couldn't believe how close they came to me—about twenty feet. Then two more deer followed in their tracks. They stopped and looked at me for over a minute and then walked on. It was a "high" that only a deer hunter could appreciate. I felt so close to God as I was talking to Him and now, at that moment, here were some of His creation to thrill me. I was so excited; I couldn't wait to tell my wife and Charlie. I rushed home with enthusiasm. When I got home, I was told that the hospital had called. Dad had suffered a major heart attack that afternoon. I had intended to go to the hospital that evening, but now it was an emergency, and I needed to go right away. As I look back on that experience with the deer, I know God caused that interlude to encourage my heart. It was like a breath of fresh air because I was really down and discouraged with a heavy heart. My God still supplies all of my needs—physically, emotionally, mentally, and spiritually.

Jackie and I immediately drove those seventy miles to the hospital to be with my mother and sister. Dad's body was loaded down with tubes everywhere as he lay in ICU. His kidneys were failing. His heart was weak. The bed sheet was pulled up to his chin, and he was on a respirator. A registered nurse sat next to his bed, monitoring all of the machines. The surgeon had warned us before the operation that several things could happen; he could hemorrhage, he could have a heart attack, or his kidneys could fail. All three things happened.

Every so often, we could go into ICU to see Dad, and the rest of the time, we just waited down the hall in that waiting room. The doctor said that he could linger on for some time, so it was difficult for me to know what to do about keeping an appointment to preach the following morning at the Hornell Baptist Church.

About 10:30 p.m., I decided to go home and prepare myself to preach the following morning. This was very difficult, knowing that my father was probably dying seventy miles away. I told my mother to call me if there were any changes in Dad's condition. I walked into the ICU one last time to say goodbye. I don't know if he heard me, but I told him one last time that I loved him and that one day, we would meet again. Jackie and I arrived home at midnight, and as I walked in the door, the telephone was ringing. I immediately knew that it was the call that I never wanted to get. Dad had just passed on to his heavenly reward. I never experienced such an emotional load. I knew this would happen sometime but please, Lord, not now. I tried to prepare myself for this, but one can never be totally prepared. I cried until there were no more tears to cry. I was happy for Dad, but I was sorry for myself and Mother.

Being the oldest child, I had some responsibilities to work on regarding Dad's funeral and the welfare of my Mother. As soon as I received the call of Dad's passing, I called my son, Rick, and asked him to take my preaching engagement the following morning. He was so kind to fill in for me with such short notice and under such circumstances. I stayed up most of that night praying, thinking, and planning. Dad had asked me many years before to preach at his funeral. Mother told Dad that he should not put that kind of pressure on me, and I agreed with her. I just didn't think I could ever do it. That night, while I started planning the funeral, I thought of Dad's request, and suddenly I realized that I must preach at his funeral because there were some things that needed to be said about my Dad that only I could say.

I opened the first Bible Dad got after trusting Christ as his Savior. It was well worn, with pages soiled from heavy usage and all kinds of notes written in the columns. While leafing through the pages, I came across a poem that I had written and given to Dad on June 19, 1977, more than a year before he died. Mother told me how much Dad cherished it and that he carried it in his Bible. I wrote this one evening to express my grateful thoughts to Dad:

Dear Dad:

I have many fond memories of early years,
As you tenderly guided me through childhood fears.

Your wisdom and counsel and genuine love
Brought me to the point where I feared God above.

I trusted in Him because I knew you did,
And now I rejoice too because my sins are hid.

There came to my life a desire and a thirst
To serve my dear Lord and always give to Him first.

To you, I am grateful for being my Dad.
Your example helped me for the sons I had.

I'll always be grateful for what you gave me—
A heritage, a faith and how to be free.

God bless you, dear Dad, as you keep helping me
To preach Jesus Christ and help sinners get free.

Your reward, I know it will really be great,
Since you've led so many through those pearly gates.

Love, your son, Dick

The day after Dad died, Jimmy Cleland, who was a dear friend, a retired businessman from Prattsburgh, and a generous volunteer at YFC, came by the house to extend his sympathies. I will never forget his encouraging words as he said, "I'll be your dad now, Dick." Jim and Doris Cleland had been full-time volunteers at YFC for years. They were associated with us from the very first year and had been faithful supporters in many ways. Jim treated me like a son in many ways. When they moved to Florida, he asked me if I would take care of Doris if anything should happen to him. He gave me a list of his assets and a copy of his will. Years later, when he died, I knew I had a new responsibility. Doris began telling everybody that I was her son. I felt much honored, but at times it was confusing, and she had to explain that I was her adopted son.

Dad's funeral service was held at the Family Life Center. I led the service, accompanied by several pastors. When I stood up to begin my message, I struggled with my emotions. However, once I got through the first two or three sentences, I was able to share my love for my Dad because of his love for His Lord. A second service was held in Calvary Church in Lancaster the following day. David Barr, a representative of the Billy Graham organization and a friend of Dad's, preached at the second service. Dad was buried in the Willow Street Mennonite Church graveyard next to my brother, Jimmy. Dad was not a perfect man, but he loved God, he loved people, and he loved to spread God's message of salvation. One of the greatest things I ever heard my sons say about my dad was "Regardless of who Grandpa talks to, sooner or later, the conversation is about Jesus." What a heritage. Thank you, Lord. *"For to whomsoever much is given, of him shall be much required"* (Luke 12:48 KJV).

TO MOTHER—A REAL SAINT OF GOD

Mother was just as great in exemplifying her Christianity as Dad was, only she was not nearly as vocal. In her quiet way, she made an impact upon my life that I could never forget. It was many years after I was involved in Christian ministry that my mother told me that she had dedicated me to the Lord's service when I was born, and she prayed that I would become a minister of the Gospel. Wow! What a heritage.

The best way to describe my Mother is to call her a saint. She was a soft-spoken lady with a very tender heart. She was a hard worker who was kind and went out of her way to help others. She never complained. She was a real help-meet to my Dad wherever he went and whatever he did. She was a great wife, mother, and grandmother. I loved her dearly.

After Dad died, Mother moved into a senior citizens apartment complex in Bath. She was loved and respected by all of the residents. She refused to take sides when problems came up among the residents, and she was kind and patient with everyone.

Her patience was demonstrated one time when I took her to her doctor at the Guthrie Clinic in Sayre, PA. The doctor gave her a prescription for some much-needed pain medication. We hurried back to her apartment, and I went to the drug store to get the prescription filled. I was dismayed when the pharmacist refused to fill the prescription because it was for a controlled substance. The doctor at Guthrie mistakenly wrote the prescription on a Pennsylvania form, making it necessary for a Pennsylvania pharmacy to fill it. I knew that I had to make a trip to Pennsylvania and find a drug store before they closed for the day. I went back to the apartment, got her settled in a chair and told her to wait for me to return with the pain medication.

The closest route to the Pennsylvania border was south on US Route 15, and the border town was Lawrenceville. I arrived in Lawrenceville, only to discover that there was no pharmacy in that town. The next town south was Tioga, PA. It was dark when I arrived in Tioga, only to find no pharmacy. I was frustrated, knowing that my Mother was sitting in a chair in Bath in a great deal of pain. I checked the phone book to discover that there was a pharmacy in Wellsboro, so I headed west. It was now dark, and it began to snow. The roads became very slippery, and visibility was almost zero in that blizzard. I knew that I had to get there before they closed, so I prayed for my Mother and for safety as I drove.

It was dark and the snow was accumulating rapidly as I drove into the parking lot of the pharmacy in Wellsboro. I was so glad to see lights on in the store, assuring me that they were still open. The pharmacist filled the prescription, and I hurried out to my car to begin the snowy, slippery road back to Bath. I quickly rushed up the stairs and down the hall to Mother's apartment and found her still sitting in that same chair patiently waiting for me. She forced a smile through her pain as I entered her room. For three hours, that dear woman patiently waited in pain and prayed for me as I was on my mission. She didn't complain for the long wait. She didn't question why it took so long. She just thanked me and expressed her appreciation.

Mother had heart problems for several years and, after suffering two heart attacks, the doctor informed me that she needed special and constant nursing care. I was frustrated because I knew Jackie and I could not meet her medical and nursing care needs. I contacted numerous nursing care facilities, but because of her very limited resources, there was no room available. She remained in the hospital for several days while I tried to find help. Out of the blue, my dear cousin, Arlene Mellinger, called and said that she had heard of her Aunt Anna's need for nursing care. Arlene worked in the Admissions Department at Landis Homes in Lancaster, PA, and she said that a bed was open at Landis Homes and she would hold it for Mother if I got her there the next day. This was a tremendous answer to prayer and just when needed. The doctor approved the trip to Lancaster, and we made the trip the following day. Mother slept most of the way and didn't remember ever taking the trip. As I drove up to the Landis Homes facility, two of her sisters were there to meet her— my Aunt Marian LeFever and Aunt Erma Buckwalter. Mother felt at home in this Mennonite facility and spent the remainder of her life at Landis Homes.

We visited Mother numerous times, and each time we thought that it might be the last one. Her eyes were failing so that she could not read or do needle work, so she just sat in her chair during the day with a smile, waiting for that heavenly call. Twelve years after Dad died, Mother joined him in heaven on July 3, 1990. I received a call from my brother, Glenn, informing me of her passing. That same day of her death, I sat down and wrote the following tribute to my mother:

To her family and friends,
Anna was her name.
To me it was plain "Mother,"
And that was her great fame.

She gave me back to God
Soon after I was born,
That I would serve the Savior,
Through times of good and storm.

She loved and cared and prayed,
And taught me at her knee,
That I would grow into
A man of great integrity.

To mom her life and Godly walk,
Were samples of love,
On how to live with man on earth,
And then with God above.

Her smile and little twinkle
She freely gave to all,
Will long be remembered
By all who came to call.

No complaints or bad words
Of others did she say,
She just enjoyed her friends,
And family each day.

Often she was quiet, unseen
And "matter of fact,"
But her Godly life on all
Has made a great impact.

Today she left her body,
Old and weak and worn,
After completing God's purpose
For which she was born.

Anna was her name,
To many far and wide
But to me she was "Mother,"
And all that name implied.

Glenn made the funeral arrangements. The funeral was held in the chapel at Landis Homes, and burial was at the Willow Street Mennonite cemetery.

14

❧ ❧

THE FUTURE

As God opens doors in the future for FLM to minister, our prayer is that we will move forward in His timing and with His blessing. This has been a ministry of many miracles, financially and spiritually. Thousands of young people and many adults began their spiritual journey with Jesus Christ here at FLM. Many of their children and their grandchildren are following in their footsteps as well. Hundreds of these have gone on to serve the Lord on the mission field, in the pastorate, or in some other type of full-time Christian service. Never did we dream, nearly fifty years ago, that one day FLM would be a witness around the world through world missions and radio Internet broadcasting. God had a plan, and He continues to work His plan when we allow Him to work in us and through us for His glory.

The future of this ministry is in God's hands. It has been an honor and privilege to have served the Lord at Family Life Ministries since 1957. The board of directors has been so gracious and generous to me and my family; however, I knew the time would come when I needed to step aside and welcome a new leader. For several years, I encouraged the board of directors to search for a successor, as I felt it was soon time for younger blood to lead this organization on to new heights. After much prayer and evaluation of some prospects, I was happy when they decided that my son, Rick, appeared to have the leadership qualities to direct this organization.

In 2002, I announced to the board and staff that I was resigning (not retiring) my leadership position as President/CEO of FLM. This was a very difficult decision and was accompanied by many mixed emotions, but this difficult decision was made more palatable knowing that my son, Rick, would be my successor. Rick was then appointed the new President and CEO of Family Life Ministries, Inc. The board wanted me to stay involved and gave me the title and responsibilities of Chief Financial Officer. Jackie and I plan to continue working at FLM so long as God grants us good health. My prayer is that we all may be found faithful in every aspect until Jesus comes. To God be all the glory for what He has done for me and in me and through me. He alone is worthy to be praised.

MY LEGACY

As I reminisce about the past fifty years, I am humbled and grateful for what God did in and through just an ordinary guy. First and foremost, I am grateful for a faithful, caring, and loving wife who stuck by me for over fifty-four years. Secondly, I am grateful and thankful for our children. Carol Ann is married to Roger Book, and they live in the Atlanta, Georgia area, where she is a special projects manager and real estate broker. Carol Anne and Roger have two children. Rick, who has gone on to become President/CEO of FLM, is married to Sherri, and they also have two children. Their son, Chad, is on staff in the radio and music department. He is the third generation at FLM. Randy is the preacher of the family and the sports announcer on FLM. He and his wife, Kris, have four children. Ron, a local attorney, is married to Pam. They have three children.

My children all benefited much growing up in this ministry. They personally witnessed the many miracles, spiritual victories, and wonders that God performed in answer to our prayers over the years. They prayed with us when we had financial needs and gave thanks when God miraculously provided. They prayed when I was faced with a big decision and were excited to see how God worked it out. They prayed when they knew that I was counseling a parent or teenager. I was blessed to be able to share the many things that I learned in working with teenagers with my own children. They have applied these experiences and truths in their own lives and today they are walking with the Lord and serving Him. I can't think of a greater legacy. I am most grateful and deeply humbled.

I echo the sentiments of King David... *"O God, you have helped me from my earliest childhood and I have constantly testified to others of the wonderful things you do."* (Psalm 71:17 LB).

I AM BLESSED, and I can say with King David... *"I will tell everyone how great and good you are; I will praise you all day long"* (Psalm 35:28 LB).

"O Lord, you alone are my hope; I've trusted you from childhood. Yes, you have been with me from birth and have helped me constantly—no wonder I am always praising you! My success—at which so many stand amazed—is because you are my mighty protector. All day long I'll praise and honor you, O God, for all that you have done for me" (Psalm 71:5-8 LB).

Just an ordinary guy... with the extraordinary God!

TO GOD BE THE GLORY,
GREAT THINGS HE HAS DONE...
GREAT THINGS HE IS DOING...
AS LONG AS WE GLORIFY HIM,
GREAT THINGS HE WILL CONTINUE TO DO...

"The main end of life is not to do but to become."
F. B. Meyer

TO CONTACT THE AUTHOR

P.O. Box 38, Avoca, NY 14809
dicksnavely@fln.org
www.fln.org